Dadeland Mall
Miami, FL

Contents

Page 1: Chen Design Associates
Previous Spread: Lorenc + Yoo Design
Opposite Page: Evenson Design Group
Following Page: Ross Creative + Strategy

Remarks: We extend our heartfelt thanks to contributors throughout the world who have made it possible to publish a wide and international spectrum of the best work in this field. Entry instructions for all Graphis Books may be requested from: Graphis Inc., 307 Fifth Avenue, Tenth Floor, New York, New York 10016, or visit our web site at www.graphis.com.

Anmerkungen: Unser Dank gilt den Einsendern aus aller Welt, die es uns ermöglicht haben, ein breites, internationales. Spektrum der besten Arbeiten zu veröffentlichen. Teilnahmebedingungen für die Graphis-Bücher sind erhältlich bei: Graphis, Inc., 307 Fifth Avenue, Tenth Floor, New York, New York 10016. Besuchen Sie uns im World Wide Web, www.graphis.com.

Remerciements: Nous remercions les participants du monde entier qui ont rendu possible la publication de cet ouvrage offrant un panorama complet des meilleurs travaux. Les modalités d'inscription peuvent être obtenues auprès de: Graphis, Inc., 307 Fifth Avenue, Tenth Floor, New York, New York 10016. Rendez-nous visite sur notre site web: www.graphis.com.

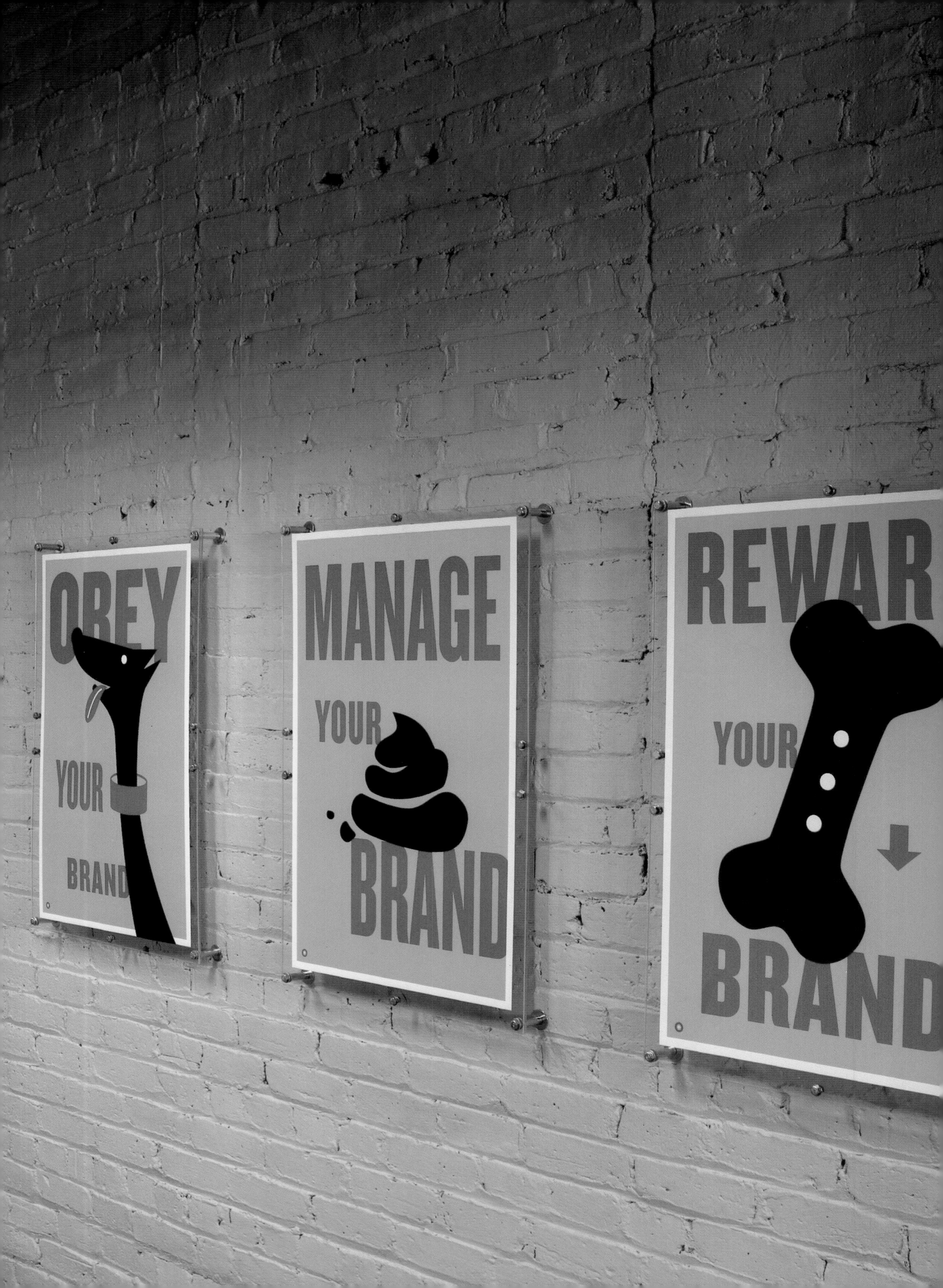
OBEY
YOUR
BRAND
MANAGE
YOUR
BRAND
REWAR
YOUR
BRAND

What does your corporate brand say to your customers?

Does it communicate to your customers exactly the message you wish to convey?

Whether your brand is used to market products and services or build a corporate perception or vision, a successful branding strategy will create, implement, and open a corporate communications-to-client dialogue that is clear, precise and focused.

BrandingUSA No. 2 presents a cross-section of the top branding designers and firms in the U.S. Their clientele consists of an equally diverse cross-section of American business, from major players to start-ups. What these designers all have in common, however, is a successful track record for creating and implementing some of the most innovative branding strategies.

The branding firms featured here present, in their own words, their own corporate branding philosophy, and with beautifully reproduced, full-color images, they showcase some of their most successful branding projects.

As you read through this volume, take a moment to appreciate the variety of design directions that these top-notch branding professionals have used to solve the multitude of problems encountered in overcoming their clients' branding problems. Each design firm may have approached and satisfied their clients' needs differently, but there can be no questioning the successful end-result of their branding efforts.

Read, study, and enjoy this volume, for nowhere else is collected so many excellent examples of branding executions from branding experts at branding firms both large and small.

BrandingUSA No. 2 is your tour guide across America, with stops along the way at some of the finest branding firms in existence today. They share portfolios of their most important work, they explain their design/branding philosophy, and you don't have to leave your home or office to visit. Just turn the pages, learn and enjoy the trip. And, as a bonus, just think of the money you'll save on gas!

We create positive change— in our clients' growth, meaning of their brands, and relationships with their audiences—to make the world a healthier place.

Addis Creson is an unusual breed of brand and design consultancy that partners with clients who have the courage to redefine the categories in which they compete and the idealism to improve the world.

ADDIS CRESON

2515 Ninth Street, Berkeley, California 94710   510.704.7500   addiscreson.com

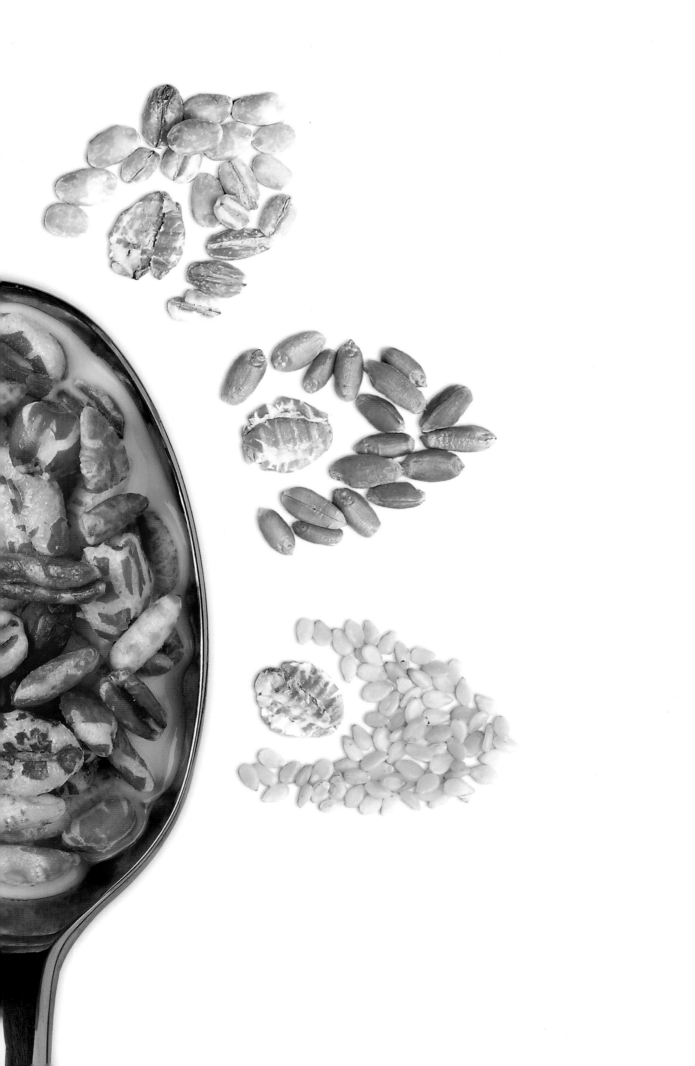

Kashi

Our deep, long-term relationship with Kashi is a partnership truly based on shared values. Over the past five years, our work together has touched all aspects of Kashi's branding, succeeding in positioning Kashi as the healthy lifestyle leader, well beyond the cereal aisle.

BRAND STRATEGY
NAMING
ARCHETYPAL ANALYSIS
CORPORATE IDENTITY SYSTEM
BRAND IDENTITY SYSTEMS
PACKAGING SYSTEMS

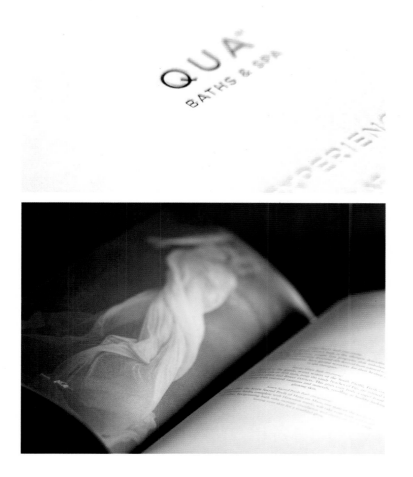

**Qua Baths & Spa
at Caesars Palace**

As non-gaming revenue has
surpassed gaming revenue, there
is tremendous focus on creating
entertainment and lifestyle brands.
Beginning with its Las Vegas flagship,
Caesars tasked us to create its
global spa brand. Our work shuns
the typical spa imagery—from the
name to our striking photography
depicting the sensual effects of
water. By courageously breaking
with the trite norms of spa branding,
Qua Baths & Spa gained instant
recognition, while also contemporiz-
ing the image of the Caesars brand.

BRAND STRATEGY
NAMING (Qua)
NOMENCLATURE SYSTEM
IDENTITY SYSTEM
COLLATERAL SYSTEM
PACKAGING SYSTEM
WEBSITE

Kidfresh

Realizing every parent's challenge
to conveniently prepare healthy,
fresh meals for today's kids gave
our entrepreneurial client his "eureka"
moment—create a grocery store
dedicated to the nutritional needs
of kids and provide peace-of-mind
and convenience for parents.

BRAND STRATEGY
IDENTITY SYSTEM
PACKAGING SYSTEM
ENVIRONMENTAL DESIGN

GE Healthcare

NAMING (Beyond)
COLLATERAL

Intel

BRAND STRATEGY
IDENTITY SYSTEM
CO-BRANDING ARCHITECTURE
BROADCAST ANIMATION

Think Products

BRAND STRATEGY
PACKAGING SYSTEM
WEBSITE

Turn, Inc.

BRAND STRATEGY
NAMING (Turn)
IDENTITY SYSTEM
WEBSITE

BriteSmile

BRAND STRATEGY
IDENTITY SYSTEM
PACKAGING SYSTEM

ADDIS CRESON

2515 Ninth Street
Berkeley, California 94710
510.704.7500
addiscreson.com

Alexander Isley Inc.
9 Brookside Place
Redding, CT 06896
203.544.9692
www.alexanderisley.com

We are experts in brand development and communication design for organizations involved with culture, fashion, and architecture.

We work with companies and institutions to help craft their brand personalities and introduce them to the public. Our teams of designers, writers, and strategists work among all disciplines to establish a consistent voice, attitude, and point of view to position our clients in the minds of their audience. This is important because, as with people, organizations are judged by what they say, how they look, and the way they behave. (We can do a lot to help with the first two.)

Our nine-person firm, founded in 1988, has received recognition and numerous awards in the fields of corporate identity, marketing communications, publication design, architectural signage, retail merchandising, packaging, and exhibit design.

As an important part of our practice, we utilize our expertise in sustainable, environmentally friendly and socially responsible design. In so doing, we work in collaboration with our clients to create work that reflects and advances their mission and values. Our clients want to do the right things, and so do we.

Our team has created effective and memorable work for a diverse range of clients including A|X Armani Exchange, *Weekly Reader*, The Rock and Roll Hall of Fame and Museum, Brooklyn Academy of Music, the Robin Hood Foundation, iVillage, Scholastic, French Toast School Uniforms, Starbucks, and the National Endowment for the Arts.

While the work our firm undertakes is quite varied, our approach to solving problems is consistent: Do the research, establish an appropriate plan of action, and, above all, always determine what something should do before thinking about what it should look like. We then produce a solution that is direct, appropriate, and memorable.

This approach has worked well, as we at Alexander Isley Inc. have earned the trust of our clients while gaining an international reputation for innovative, influential, and effective work.

Stone Barns Center for Food and Agriculture
Pocantico Hills, NY

Stone Barns Center is an innovative farm, restaurant, and educational facility promoting sustainable farm-to-table agricultural initiatives. We developed a comprehensive communications, outreach, identity, and signage program and were instrumental in the positioning and launch of the facility, which is situated on an 80-acre compound that is part of the Rockefeller family estate. Our ongoing involvement includes the creation of printed materials produced with paper manufactured using electricity provided by wind energy. Even the note cards are sustainable: They contain carrot or lettuce seeds—just plant them and they grow.

Architects: Machado and Silvetti

HARVEST FEST
Stone Barns Center
for Food and Agriculture

JOIN US!

Saturday, October 1, 2005
10 am–4 pm rain or shine
Admission $15 per car

Jay & Molly
lead an old-fashioned barn
dance in the courtyard

ALONG WITH
farm tours, farm
olympics, bake-off,
and children's
activities

Zydeco music by
The Gotham Playboys
Bluegrass music by
Fiddler's Bridge
Jug music by
The Jug Addicts

Hayrides,
music,
games, and
goodies for
the family

Community Market
and A Taste of the Farm 12 pm–4 pm
In the courtyard

630 Bedford Road
Pocantico Hills, NY
914 366 6200
www.stonebarnscenter.org

STONE BARNS CENTER FOR FOOD & AGRICULTURE

Stora Enso
Stamford, CT

We created sales materials promoting Centura, a premium-grade FSC-certified paper. Stora Enso has for nine years running been listed on the Dow Jones Sustainability Index and recently received the highest possible score (100%) in environmental reporting and policy. Our mission was to show how a premium paper can be produced and distributed using
sustainable best practices, and we set out to demonstrate that such an undertaking doesn't have to be strident or preachy and that the message can be conveyed with wit and spirit. In positioning Centura as "better than best," we wrote and produced a memorable series of over-the-top parody brochures aimed at the travel, education, and real estate markets.

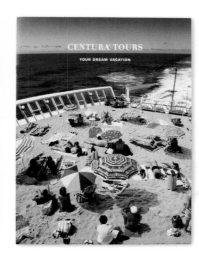

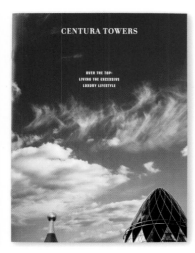

The Actors' Fund
New York, NY

We created the overall marketing and communications
program for an innovative philanthropy that supports
people in the entertainment industry. The Actors' Fund has
been a vital force in the lives of performers since its
founding in 1882. We were brought in to create a new
communications strategy and to design outreach materials
in order to better position them in the minds of their
stakeholders and potential sponsors. The program has
served to reinvigorate the institution and better spread
their good word in a memorable way.

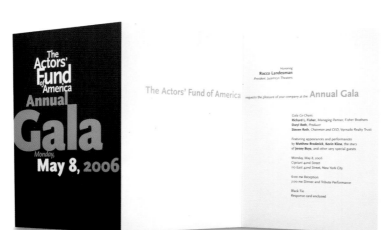

1

Vh1 Save the Music foundation

2

VH1 Save the Music Foundation
New York, NY

We designed a new visual identity on the occasion of the
foundation's tenth anniversary. The VH1 Save the Music
Foundation is a national organization that provides
musical instruments to urban public schools, with the
knowledge that kids who perform music do better
in school and have higher confidence and self-esteem.
The wordmark was developed to incorporate a trumpet,
a key element of the previous identity, providing a
refined, evolutionary approach.

1 Logo: After

2 Logo: Before

Chevron Technology Ventures
Houston, TX

We were commissioned to develop an overview and capabilities booklet for a division of the Chevron Corporation that funds and encourages research and development of alternative energy solutions. The design incorporates a narrative brochure and an editable system in which updated case studies can be added. The piece was produced using environmentally friendly practices and materials.

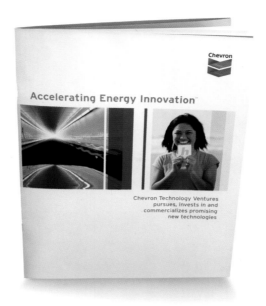

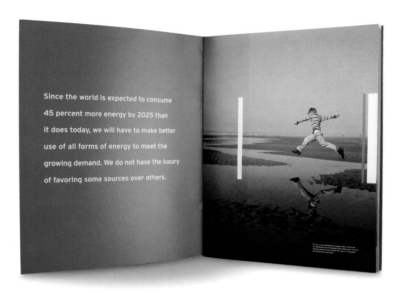

We were commissioned to create a comprehensive identity program for this groundbreaking, eco-friendly, LEED-certified residential development on New York's Roosevelt Island. We produced communications materials, advertising, a Website, and architectural signage. The development has received awards from the EPA and the Department of Environmental Protection for its incorporation of sustainable materials and practices. In planning our work, we made sure that our approach adhered to the same standards and philosophy.

Architects: Becker + Becker

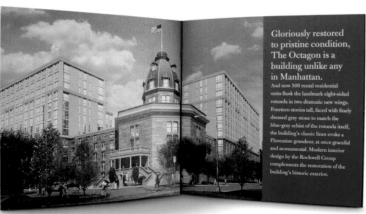

Gloriously restored to pristine condition, The Octagon is a building unlike any in Manhattan.

And now 500 rental residential units flank the landmark eight-sided rotunda in two dramatic new wings. Fourteen stories tall, faced with finely dressed gray stone to match the blue-gray schist of the rotunda itself, the building's classic lines evoke a Florentine grandeur, at once graceful and monumental. Modern interior design by the Rockwell Group complements the restoration of the building's historic exterior.

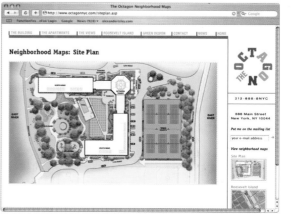

U.S. Green Building Council
Washington, DC

As part of our work with the USGBC, the leading advocacy agency for sustainable architecture in the United States, we developed outreach and communication materials—including registration documents, advertising, and attendees' guides for the national Greenbuild Conference; a trade show exhibit; and an enrollment campaign targeting architecture students.

ARGUS is an internationally recognized design agency with a primary focus on developing and integrating branded design applications. We translate the value of our clients' products and services in ways that influence the purchasing decisions of their customers.

In short, we greatly strengthen our clients' business value by expertly bringing clear, compelling messages to life through a variety of means:

. Brand Development

. Naming

. Design

No matter what form the final product takes—from identity to print, packaging to environment or interactive—we are dedicated to making our clients' brands more memorable, and to making their investment in effective communications a valuable strategy for improving business.

351 N
Second
San Fra
415.24
www.ar

Make-

TOKYObay

COMPOUND
SEMICONDUCTOR
SUBSTRATES

SOLAR

a x t i
NASDAQ: AXTI

Power Integrations
2003 Annual Report

we're
cleaning
up

Household products powered by integrated
circuits from the Power Integrations:

Vacuum cleaners, rice cookers, electric toys,
electric clippers, electric toothbrushes.

Building and industrial products
powered by our ICs:

Power tools, lighting systems,
security systems, motor controls,
industrial controls, uninterruptible
power supplies

and
building

THIS PAGE, TOP TO BOTTOM

Tokyo Bay
Fashion Accessories
Packaging

Fong & Fong Wine
Packaging

Billington Wines
Wine Maker and Importer
Havens Wine Cellars
Brochure

FACING PAGE

Billington Wines
Wine Maker and Importer
Billington Wine Studio
Brochure

IT'S
IN
THE
BOTTLE

do.

BILLINGTON
WINE
STUDIO

BUILDING   SUSTAINING   LEADING

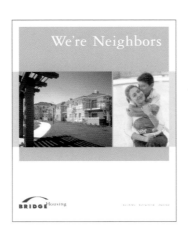

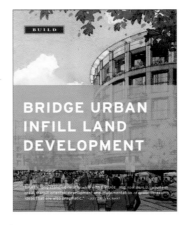

Our **MISSION** is to enable families and individuals of all income levels to obtain quality housing and become homeowners by providing wholesale products and services that help member financial institutions expand the availability of mortgage credit, compete more effectively in their markets, and foster strong and vibrant communities.

"We bring credit home."

home

power

FEDERAL HOME LOAN BANK OF SAN FRANCISCO 2007 ANNUAL REPORT

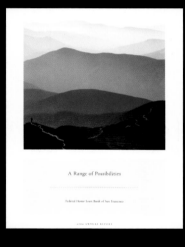

A Range of Possibilities

Federal Home Loan Bank of San Francisco

2004 ANNUAL REPORT

Federal Home Loan Bank of San Francisco

2003 ANNUAL REPORT

a system that WORKS

Federal Home Loan Bank of San Francisco 2008 ANNUAL REPORT

We're Here For You

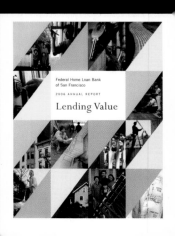

Federal Home Loan Bank of San Francisco

2006 ANNUAL REPORT

Lending Value

BAKER

Baker | Brand Communications
1424 Lincoln Boulevard
Santa Monica, CA 90401
800.939.5008

www.bakerbuilds.com

Baker is a corporate brand consultancy and communications design firm. For nearly 25 years we've been helping corporations achieve their business objectives and market potential through strategically grounded, creatively driven communications. Baker's award-winning strategists, writers, designers and dedicated account teams draw upon proven methodologies and offer clients a superior level of service. Our comprehensive communications services include brand strategy and development, identity systems and naming, corporate communications, annual reports, marketing communications, interactive, video/media and brand management. We are headquartered in Santa Monica, California, with satellite offices in Denver, Colorado and Cincinnati, Ohio.

Cephalon

Brand Strategy and Development
Identity Refresh
Tagline
Visual and Verbal Expression
Brand Photography Library
Internal Launch
External Launch
Usage Guidelines
Annual Reports
Advertising
Branded Environments
Corporate Communications
Marketing Communications
Websites
Motion Graphics
Video

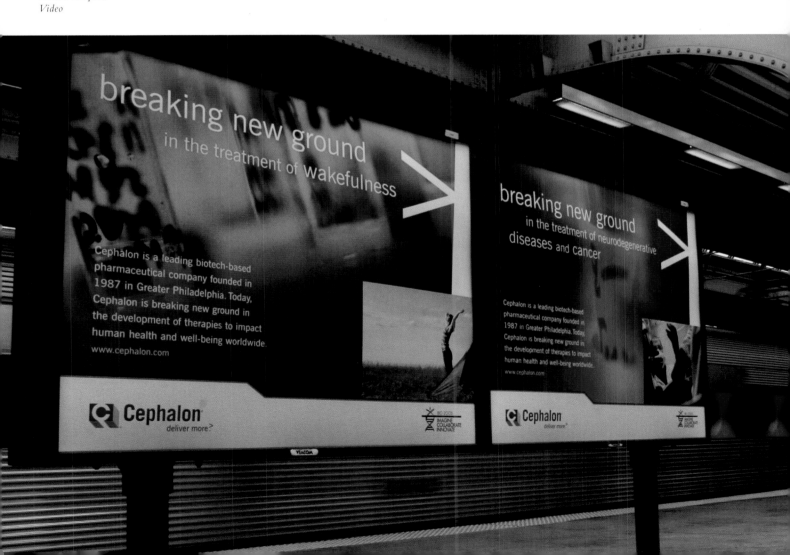

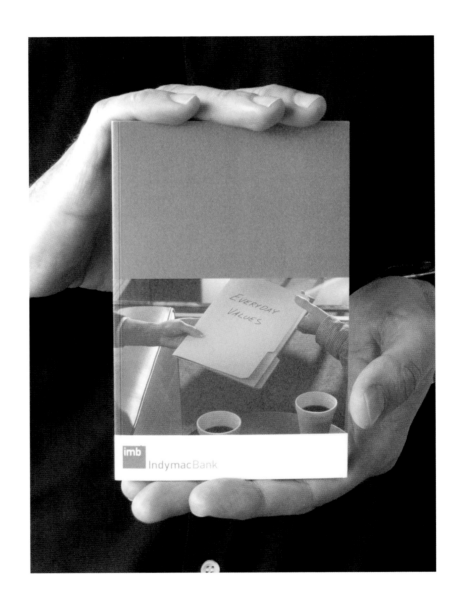

Indymac Bank
Values Program

Strategy and Development
Messaging
Handbook
Website
Email Campaign
Posters

CAN YOU
SEE THEM?

THEY'RE **HERE.**

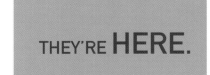

OUR VALUES: KEYS TO
EXTRAORDINARY SUCCESS

Telepan Restaurant

Brand Identity
Collateral
Website
Posters

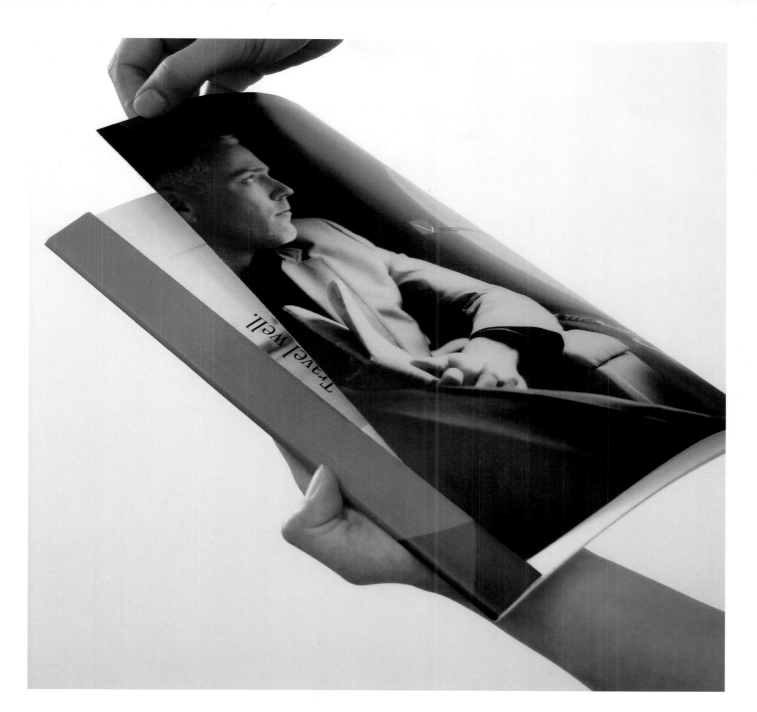

Maguire Aviation

Brand Strategy and Development
Brand Identity
Tagline
Visual and Verbal Expression
Brand Photography Library
Advertising
Signage
Branded Environments
Uniforms
Collateral
Website

International Public Relations Association
Maguire Aviation
Watson Pharmaceuticals
LA Waterfront
Nventa

Belyea
1809 7th Avenue
Suite 1250
Seattle, WA 98101
206.682.4895
www.belyea.com

cultivate

Belyea partners with ambitious companies to tell compelling stories and build authentic brands.

We believe good branding is genuine and hardworking, consistent and clear. It should feel a bit like deja vu, like a realization of what you always knew but couldn't quite identify. We discover your brand's hidden strengths and position you for success.

Our marketing programs are crafted to resonate with your target audience and generate transactions. We use strategy, messaging and design to capture the audience's attention and move your organization forward.

PROMIUM | *Laboratory Software Company*

*This identity and collateral project conveys the value
of the brand with messaging and imagery focused on the
environmental testing industry.*

*Project Scope: Identity, Business Papers, Folder, Product Sheets,
Packaging, Website and Trade Show Graphics*

PRŌMIUM
The environmental LIMS company

We speak
the language
of your lab

PRŌMIUM
The environmental LIMS company

Murthy Kalkura (MK)
Chief Operating Officer

mk@promium.com

CEL 425.466.6859
PH 425.286.9200
FX 425.286.9201

promium.com

22522 29th Dr SE, Suite 205
Bothell, WA 98021

PEMCO INSURANCE | *Regional Insurance Company*

Developed to energize PEMCO's human resources, the go! program's elements are playful and unexpected.

Project Scope: Identity, Usage Standards, Brochure, Intranet Interfaces, Banners and Promotional Items

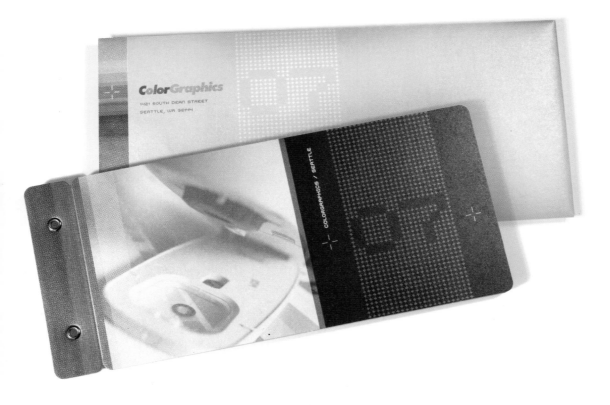

YOU CAN'T PUT A **FRENCH FOLD** ON A PDF

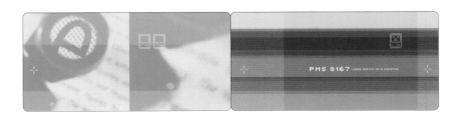

PMS 8167 LOOKS PRETTY ON A PRINTER

IT'S MORE THAN JUST INK ON PAPER. **PRINT IS REAL.**

HERE'S TO ANOTHER YEAR OF KEEPING IT REAL.

ColorGraphics

AN ELECTRONIC ANNUAL REPORT HAS **NO PRESENCE.**

COLORGRAPHICS | *Premium West Coast Printer*

Conceived to communicate the power of print, this New Year's Booklet features bold messaging and a vibrant palette. The ticket-style booklet is printed with UV inks on iridescent paper.

Project Scope: Booklet and Envelope

In Harmony
sustainable landscapes

sageLISTINGS.COM

THE FEAREY GROUP

LAIRD NORTON
TYEE

CELLULOSE FIBERS
bright ideas

Glacier Bay
CRUISELINE

GeoTrust℠

PEMCO Life

vue
LODGE

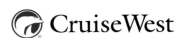

CruiseWest

Les Piafs

Prolumina
TRIAL TECHNOLOGIES

STRATEGY + MESSAGING + DESIGN

belyea.

Brainstorm
9820 Westpoint Drive
Suite 400
Indianapolis, IN 46256
brainstormbrand.com

At Brainstorm, our course is guided by a unique passion for excellence in benefit-driven solutions. Our positioning statement, "because we think harder," speaks to the fact that we think strategically on behalf of our clients in solving their communication challenges and enhancing their marketing opportunities. Our goal is to help each client accomplish outlined objectives. Whether those goals include increasing revenues, advancing efficiencies, lowering expenses or fostering new and repeat business, we always look to positively affect the quality of our clients' products and services.

Through our proprietary, strategic, market-driven process, called THINK benefit,™ we provide tangible, quantifiable results that give our clients the competitive edge. That's why *U.S. News & World Report* called Brainstorm: "a new breed of consultant." Brainstorm offers a complete approach to marketing needs that is rooted in analysis as well as creativity. Before we begin a project, we first consider what the finished product should accomplish, not simply what graphic elements it should contain. From conception to completion, our integrated, strategic design services include

corporate, brand and product identity; print collateral; multimedia presentations; web development; consumer packaging and sales collateral materials including business-to-business as well as business-to-consumer based initiatives. Our vision is to be a creative partner for our clients, to deliver innovative and effective solutions that meet every marketing challenge and to expand organizations to encompass new and limitless opportunities.

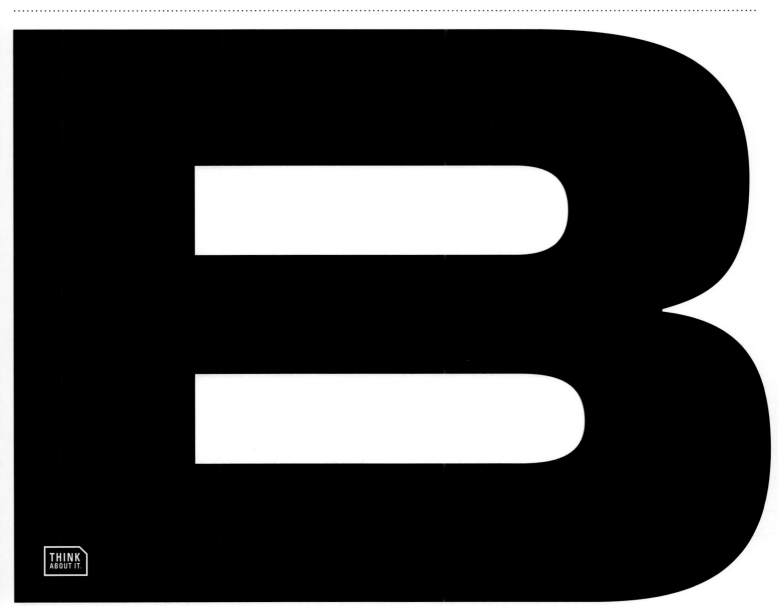

THINK ABOUT IT.

Sheila's Studio Spa
RCA

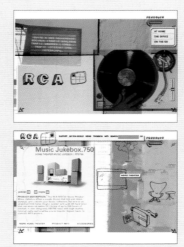

THE LATINO STORY

WHAT WE KNOW ABOUT LATINO/A STUDENT ACCESS AND SUCCESS IN POSTSECONDARY EDUCATION.

A REPORT TO THE LUMINA FOUNDATION

THE FAMILY

PARENTS + FAMILY

#33

Supportive parents and family can positively impact the educational achievements of Latino students. Support entails positive communication, good relationships with adults, a caring environment, and parents' interest in their children's education. Students from such families say that their families value academic goals, believe in their ability to contribute, provide role models, advocate for students, and provide a safe environment. Families also can provide "counter stories" that portray college going as challenging but worthwhile. Thus, families can create either a "culture of possibility" or a "culture of success" that channels the student into high educational attainment.

BACK | NEXT

PARENTS + FAMILY
CULTURE + LANGUAGE
RACE + IDENTITY
MESSAGE + RESILIENCE

THE STORY
THE REPORT
FAMILY

THE LIBRARY

Select Topic(s):

male curriculum education art family blog structure books home computer after school care daily database instructors demographics English entertainment traditions siblings friendships retention peers fun games habits career goals relationships health history home parents single home inspiration internet culture festivals holidays library symbols study habits age marketing media female movies news music technology mentors college

Select Additional Topic(s):

GO

THE LATINO STORY

THE LUMINA
THE STORY
UNIVERSIDAD MIAMI
SEARCH THE LIBRARY

Search Topics | View Bibliography List

Bryan College

"There can be no settlement of a great cause without discussion, and people will not discuss a cause until their attention is drawn to it."

We've made a difference in our students. Our students

Brightpoint

Donet

DELPHI

LIVE it

HOME KIT SA10103

SKYFi²

XM is: Over 120 XM digital channels coast to coast • The most 100% commercial-free studio • The most fun news & popular stations • Championship NFL music & sports • Listen in your car & at home • Powered anywhere in vehicles requires a Delphi receiver & antenna • satellite reception requires paid subscription

XM ONLY IN DIRECT AN DEVICES WITH THE ROYAL RECEIVER

SATELLITE RADIO

Car Charger Plus :: 992

MOTOROLA

Lyra128   cool.

Powered by RCA Lyra Wireless and a Sony 5 to 850 to Pentium and Battery... prepared to enable it work.

Lyra128

rca

Kult Law Office

CF NAPA

2787 Napa Valley Corporate Drive | Napa, California 94558 | 707.265.1891 | www.cfnapa.com

CF Napa is a full-service brand strategy and design firm located in Napa Valley, our clients and work span the world and our philosophy is based on one simple belief: Good Design is Good Business. At CF Napa we innovatively balance strategic thinking with inspired creativity to build and evolve enduring brands. Our multidisciplinary work encompasses design for packaging, structure, logo identities, marketing collateral, websites, point-of-sale and name generation.

SPERONE

LIQUORE
DI MILANO

(70 PROOF) 35% ALC/VOL 750 ML
ITALIAN LIQUEUR

VELOCE *Identity and Packaging*
WILLIAMS-SONOMA *Bundt Identity and Packaging*
NAPA VALLEY WATER CO. *Identity and Packaging*
MCCORMICK SPICES *Packaging*
COCOA PETE'S *Identity and Packaging*

GOLDEN STATE VINTNERS *Corporate Brochure*
75 WINE COMPANY *Identity and Business System*
FOSTER'S WINE ESTATES *Beringer Launch Brochure*
SARACINA VINEYARDS *Identity and Packaging*

DEMETRIA

HESPERIAN

PURPLE WINE CO. *Bex Identity and Packaging*
PURPLE WINE CO. *Bex Sales Sheet and Point-of-Sale*
NAPA VALLEY TOFFEE CO. *Identity and Packaging*
DON SEBASTIANI & SONS *Point-of-Sale*

CFNAPA
brand design

2787 NAPA VALLEY CORPORATE DR.
NAPA, CALIFORNIA 94558
CFNAPA.COM | 707 265 1891

Chen Design Associates
649 Front Street, Third Floor
San Francisco, CA 94111
415.896.5338
www.chendesign.com

Since 1991, Chen Design Associates has been helping clients find a voice to express the genuine and the necessary, the illuminating and the unexpected. Telling your best story gets your business noticed. Telling it in bold and authentic terms keeps your audience riveted. And loyal.

Our work is guided by ambitious design thinking and grounded in the particular needs of each client. We are streamlined to stay nimble and personal, even as projects increase in size and scope. Because we are experts, not egoists, we engage clients in the process to foster respect and fuel invention. Together, we move people — to explore, to wonder, to succeed.

THE NORTH FACE

Environmental Savings

TREES

WATER

ENERGY

An annual audit will be featured
on our hang tags highlighting
the amount of trees, water, and
energy saved by printing on
recycled paper.

THIS NEW SYSTEM BETTI

OUR TECHNOLOGICAL LEA

OUTDOOR INDUSTRY, IT I

BY OUR DESIRE TO STRIV

ENVIRONMENTAL SUSTAI

ROCK 22

THE NORTH FACE

CAPACITY CAPACITÉ	SIZE DIMENSIONS	TRAIL WEIGHT JUSQ. SOLIFL
2	7' 0" X 4' 11" 3 X 5 m	4 lbs 7 oz 3 kg

ATERPROOF · BREATHABLE

The North Face

Hang Tag System
& Packaging Redesign

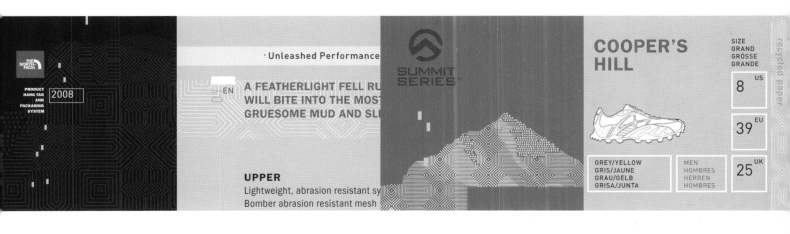

Soma Grand Lifestyle Condos

Brand Development
Sales Brochure
Direct Mail
Advertising
Identity System
Sales Center Signage

www.somagrand.com

soma grand

The sweeping views from Soma Grand span the San Francisco sun belt, from the City Hall dome to the Oakland Hills, the downtown skyline to the San Bruno Mountains. Each vista continues to expand from the awe-inspiring first residential level to the upper floors, where panoramic bay and city landmark views seem to stretch to the horizon. From here you can see forever.

Soma Grand
3 Bedroom
2 Bath

Features

- STUDIO BECKER CABINETS
  Dark Wenge And Light Tone Colors
- BOSCH STAINLESS STEEL APPLIANCES
- CAMBRIA CAESAR STONE COUNTERTOPS
- HARDWOOD FLOORING
  Entry And Kitchen
- JERUSALEM LIMESTONE
  Baths
- BALCONIES
  Select Homes
- IN-HOME LAUNDRY READY
- FIBER-OPTIC WIRING

hotel-style pampering in your own home

SOMA GRAND / SERVICE

EXPERTISE

soma grand

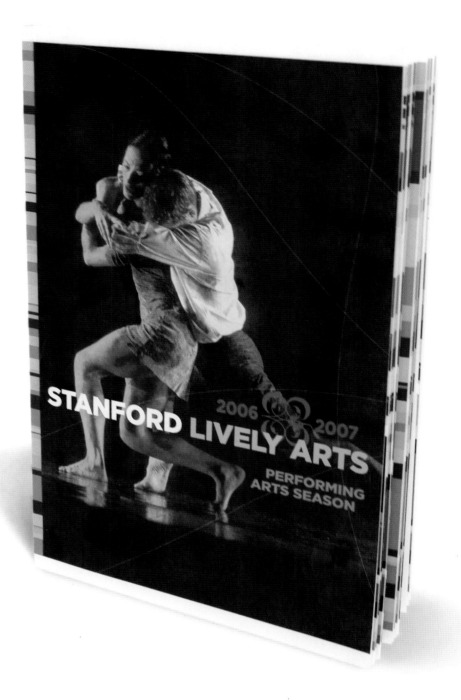

Stanford Lively Arts

Brand Development
Season Campaign
Catalog
Event Collateral
Fundraising Packet
Website

ADAMO LONDON

baker lab

CAFE LA VIE

DRAGONSLEAF

Branding & Identity

Jessica Robinson Photography
Adamo London
Baker Lab
Cafe la Vie
Dragonsleaf
Firefly Solar
Public Policy Institute of California

  PUBLIC POLICY
INSTITUTE OF CALIFORNIA

CIULLA | ASSOC.

DESIGN IS A BALANCING ACT OF DECISIONS THAT IMPACT THE BOTTOM LINE

AT CIULLA | ASSOC. WE BELIEVE THE RIGHT DESIGN DECISION IS THE STRAIGHTEST PATH TO INNOVATION

INNOVATION THAT HARNESSES THE POWER TO BREAK THROUGH

We work in the highly competitive world of brand design... not design for design sake, but design that needs to sell a product, service or philosophy. Whether consumer or corporate, design in this arena needs to balance the left and right sides of the brain on a continuous basis... constantly balancing the yin and the yang of the halls of corporate America. We understand this world and the pressure of delivering world-class design and smart strategic thinking, non-stop... it's what we do! We balance the data with the intuitive, the verbal with the visual and the logic with the emotion.

CIULLA | ASSOC. is a firm with a rich past and a promising future evolving from MLR Design's 40 year legacy in brand design and Sam Ciulla's 30 years of experience as designer, creative director and brand strategist. C | A has been transforming many of the world's most iconic brands with fresh innovative solutions that drive brand value and build deep relationships with consumers.

Our mission is to continue to evolve and be even stronger and more viable to the clients we serve and the world around us. Our vision is to be a brand design firm that bridges the best of both big and small; highly creative, innovative and true... honest to ourselves and the people we work with. Committed to partnering and collaborating with our clients, and dedicated to great service and world-class design.

MOUNT GAY RUM

MANGO

FLAVORED
BARBADOS RUM

750 ML
32% ALC./VOL.

MOUNT GAY RUM

VANILLA

FLAVORED
BARBADOS RUM

750 ML
32% ALC./VOL.

The Coca-Cola Company - Dasani   Simply Orange Juice Company - Simply Orange   The Coca-Cola Company - Kinley   PepsiCo, Inc. - Pepsi Blue

Russell Corporation - Bike Athletic Wear   Char Crust Company - Dry Rub Seasoning   The Dial Corporation - Purex Detergent   Marshall Field's - Frango Mints

The Dial Corporation - Dial Brand Revitalization

PepsiCo, Inc. - Gatorade Xtremo   Kimberly-Clark Corporation - Cottonelle Bathroom Tissue   The Dial Corporation - Pure & Natural Body Wash   Kraft Foods Global, Inc. - Oscar Mayer Bacon

Marshall Field's - Frango   Kaytee Products, Inc. - Satori Koi & Goldfish Food   Michigan Shores Club   Artisan - Shop & Gallery   Kaehler World Traveler

Pro Bono work for The J.M. Smucker Company - Heartland Point Community Center

Creativille, Inc.

Creativille, Inc.
905 Randle Street
Edwardsville, IL 62025
314.368.7365
www.creativille.net

Be Simple.
Be Passionate.
Be Creative.

Creativille, Inc. specializes
in design and brand building
for companies, institutions,
and organizations with
a unique voice.

left: New consumer product
naming, brand identity
& packaging

right: New commercial product
brand identity, roll-out
collateral & advertising

Helzberg
diamond masterpiece

Organization's re-branding,
brand identity, tagline,
& common look and feel

Institution's new
brand identity &
visual vocabulary

tion e connect

DESIGN ARMY

510 H St, NE Suite 200
Washington, DC 20002
www.designarmy.com
info@designarmy.com

Great Minds Don't Think Alike.™

DE
SIGN
ARMY

University of Virginia Library
Imagining the Future annual report

Julie Wolfe
The Birds and the Beads product portfolio

The Washington Ballet
The Beatles Ball invitation

Muléh
Modern Etiquette brochure

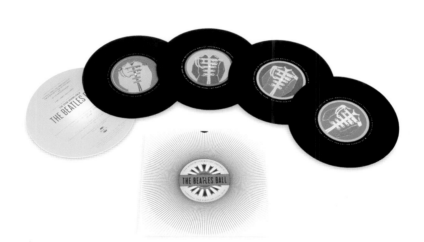

1 GEORGE WALKER BUSH

BORN: 7/6/46 Born again: 1985

NICKNAME: Dubya, Shrub, 43, The Misleader

POSITION: 43rd president of the United States of America

MISUNDERESTIMATION RATING ★★★★★

2 RICHARD BRUCE CHENEY

HATCHED: 1/30/41

NICKNAME: The Puppet Master

POSITION: 46th vice president of the United States of America

SHOTGUN ACCURACY RATING ★★☆☆☆

3 CONDOLEEZZA RICE

BORN: 11/14/54

NICKNAME: Guru

POSITION: Secretary of state

LOYALTY TO BUSH RATING ★★★★★

4 ANTONIN GREGORY SCALIA

BORN: 3/11/36

NICKNAME: Nino

POSITION: Associate justice of the Supreme Court; nominated by President Reagan

ELECTORAL HANKY PANKING RATING ★★★★☆

5 WILLIAM JAMES O'REILLY, JR. aka Bill O'Reilly

BORN: 9/10/49

NICKNAME: The Big O (Bestowed by George W. Bush), Falafel

POSITION: Host of The O'Reilly Factor since 1996, best-selling author, including The O'Reilly Factor for Kids

FAIR AND BALANCED RATING ★☆☆☆☆

6 JACK ABRAMOFF

BORN: 2/28/58

NICKNAME: Casino Jack

POSITION: Federal inmate No. 27593-112. Currently serving five years and ten months for fraud, public corruption, and tax evasion; formerly a right-wing megalobbyist.

ABUSE OF POWER RATING ★★★☆

7 KARL CHRISTIAN ROVE

BORN: 12/25/50

NICKNAME: Bush's Brain, Turd Blossom (what Bush calls him)

POSITION: Assistant to the president; senior advisor; and White House deputy chief of staff until April, 2006; thereafter, Republican election strategist

MACHIAVELLIAN RATING ★★★★★

8 RICHARD JOHN SANTORUM "Rick"

BORN: 5/10/58

NICKNAME: Rooster (thanks to unruly hair in high school)

POSITION: Former senator from Pittsburgh, Pennsylvania; forced into early retirement by voters, November 2006

LIKELINESS TO COME OUT OF CLOSET ★★★★★

9 RUSH HUDSON LIMBAUGH III

BORN: 1/12/51

NICKNAME: Rusty Sharpe, Jeff Christie (both fake radio names he has used)

POSITION: Host of The Rush Limbaugh Show, the No. 1 nationally syndicated radio talk show in the United States

HYPOCRISY RATING ★★★☆

10 ARNOLD ALOIS SCHWARZENEGGER

BORN: 7/30/47

NICKNAME: The Austrian Oak, The Governor, Conan the Republican, Herr Gröpenführe

POSITION: 38th governor of California

TIME-TRAVELING CYBORG RATING ★★★☆

11 ANN HART COULTER

BORN: 12/8/61 or 12/8/63, if you believe Ann.

NICKNAME: Coultergeist

POSITION: Author; syndicated columnist; talking head for Fox Network; pundit

ACIDITY RATING ★★★★

12 DENNIS MILLER

BORN: 11/3/53

NICKNAME: The Ranter

POSITION: Comedian; "social critic"; actor; shill for various products, including M&M's

USE OF OBSCURE REFERENCE RATING ★★★★★

13 GEORGE FELIX ALLEN

BORN: 3/8/52

NICKNAME: The Men Who Won't Be President, George of the Bungle

POSITION: Former Republican senator from Virginia

FOOT-IN-MOUTH RATING ★★★★★

14 RUDOLPH GIULIANI Rudolph William Louis Giuliani III

BORN: 5/28/44

NICKNAME: America's Mayor, Rudy the Rock

POSITION: Former mayor of New York City

TEMPER MANAGEMENT RATING ★★☆☆

15 ALBERTO R. GONZALES

BORN: 8/4/55

NICKNAME: Mr. Torture, The Judge (with White House colleagues)

POSITION: Attorney general of the United States

LOYALTY TO BUSH RATING ★★★★★

16 JOHN GLOVER ROBERTS

BORN: 1/27/55

NICKNAME: The Bland Assassin

POSITION: Chief Justice of the United States

FATHER KNOWS BEST RATING ★★★★

17 ROGER EUGENE AILES

BORN: 5/15/40

NICKNAME: The General

POSITION: Creator, and now president of, Fox News Channel

MEGALOMANIA RATING ★★★★

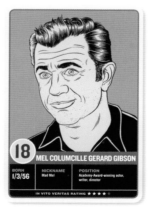

18 MEL COLUMCILLE GERARD GIBSON

BORN: 1/3/56

NICKNAME: Mad Mel

POSITION: Academy-Award-winning actor, writer, director

IN VITO VERITAS RATING ★★★☆

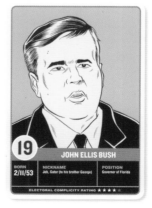

19 JOHN ELLIS BUSH

BORN: 2/11/53

NICKNAME: Jeb, Gator (to his brother George)

POSITION: Governor of Florida

ELECTORAL COMPLICITY RATING ★★★★

20 WILLIAM HARRISON FRIST, SR.

BORN: 2/22/52

NICKNAME: Fristy (courtesy of George W. Bush)

POSITION: Former U.S. Senator from Tennessee; former Senate majority leader; former presidential candidate

SHIFTY AND SHADY RATING ★★★☆

OPPOSITE
Chronicle Books
Name That Republican trivia game

TOP
**Ronald Reagan Building and
International Trade Center**
Recipes for Success direct mail campaign

**Woodrow Wilson International
Center for Scholars**
Voices of Vision annual report

RIGHT
**American Institute of Graphic Arts
Washington, D.C. Chapter**
AIGA 50 Call for Inspirations poster

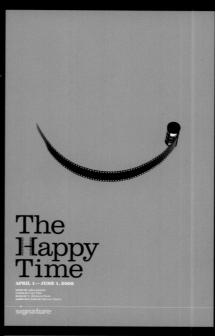

DEUTSCH DESIGN WORKS

Deutsch Design Works
10 Arkansas Street
San Francisco, CA 94107
415.487.8520

www.ddw.com

In 1995, founding partners Barry Deutsch and Lori Wynn combined creativity with strategy to generate ideas that engage and enlighten. More than a decade later, toting multiple awards and a storehouse of big-brand expertise, DDW brings forward-thinking, on-target dedication to its branding, packaging, and identity design.

Located in San Francisco's fashionable Potrero Hill district, DDW's unusual courtyard environment provides our staff of 25+ people a creative oasis. Since its inception, the lunchbox logo has symbolized the company's roots... an unpretentious, roll up your sleeves, get down to design attitude.

deutsch
DESIGN WORKS

Anheuser-Busch

DDW has partnered with Anheuser-Busch Brand Creative Services to create numerous brand marks, identities and package designs over the past decade. Our collaborative, creative relationship has produced new and redesigned brand identities and package designs for hundreds of products including the ones shown.

Intensitea

Brand Identity/
Bottle Design
3 Fruit Flavors

Bacardi Silver Mojito

Brand Identity/
Bottle Design

Budweiser

Bottle Can
Design

Budweiser Select

Crown Logo and
Bottle Can Design

Michelob Lager

Bottle Redesign
Labeling

Land Shark

Brand Identity/
Bottle Design

Anheuser-Busch Brand Creative Services requested a promotional design for the various motorcycle Bike Week events that occur around the United States each year. We created a stylized Eagle motif. The design was used on promotional materials as well as this special aluminum bottle can design.

Budweiser

Bike Week
Promotional Identity

Budweiser

Bottle Can Design
for Bike Week events

Sprint

*A line of boxes featuring
the latest and most sophisticated
technology.*

Fantastic World Foods

*This recent redesign of Fantastic's brand mark and packaging
brought to life the new positioning of "never ending discovery."
Combining stock photos for "place" and delicious food shots,
we created 65 soups, sides and meal boxes for the brand roll-out.*

Albertson's Store Brand

Essensia Fresh Fruit Pies
Package Line Design

Lipton

*Premium Iced Teas
Package Line Redesign*

Diet Pepsi

*We created the color, look and
feel for the sub-brand that became
Pepsi's flagship beverage.*

Mug Root Beer

*A redesign of Pepsi's
young male beverage –
emphasizing the product's
fun and "foamy" character.*

Bellagio Casino & Resort

*The logo design echoes the style
of an Italian lakeside town and
the luxury of Las Vegas.*

Precis Vodka

*A Swedish import bottled in
hand-blown glass and silver closure.
The name is derived from the
"precision" distillation process.*

Mondavi Winery

Talomas and Kirralaa
Brand Identity / Label Design
A cross-continental association with
Australian vintner Robert Oatley.

Doña Sol / Bronco Wines

A whimsical brand icon
combining female and sun
imagery.

Io - Byron Vineyard

A Rhone-style blend,
grown in the cool vineyards
of Santa Barbara County.

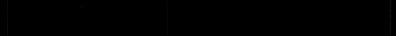

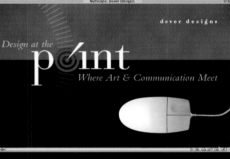

Dever Designs
14203 Park Center Dr.
Suite 308
Laurel, MD 20707

800·373·7438
www.deverdesigns.com
info@deverdesigns.com

Great design lives and breathes at the focal point of art and communication. It is the result of careful listening, creative problem-solving and artistic execution. It is on this premise that Dever Designs was founded as a multi-disciplinary design group. With studios located in the suburbs of Washington D.C. we serve clientele primarily in the mid-Atlantic region, however our award-winning design and penchant for exceptional client service have attracted a loyal clientele across North America.

At Dever Designs we believe that effective design is quality design. Design that will work hard for you and your organization. To that end

cally conceived, [...] driven materials [...] clearly project yo[...] and communicat[...] message to the ta[...] audience.

As a multi-dis[...] studio Dever De[...] talented staff offe[...] array of services. [...] our focus is on b[...] identification an[...] publication desig[...] portfolio and clie[...] are varied and di[...] This spectrum of[...] has earned Dever[...] over 500 major d[...] awards for excell[...] most important, [...] secured us a loya[...] vested clientele.

Dever Designs [...] the point where [...] communication [...]

Selections from the
award-winning annual
reports of the conservation
group, the National Fish
and Wildlife Foundation.
Used primarily as marketing
and promotional tools, the
pieces feature elegant, custom
die-cut covers and beautiful
nature photography.

Included below, a companion
invitation for an event
co-sponsored with ESPN.

Staying On Course

Will consumer privacy concerns put a dent in your company's RFID efforts?

THE PASSION OF MEL

By Clifford Goldstein

An array of covers and feature spreads from our distinguished magazine portfolio. Our diverse publications are often recognized for excellence in typography, design and illustration through various professional competitions and exhibitions.

Group Effort

Attain successful new product design by involving the entire supply chain

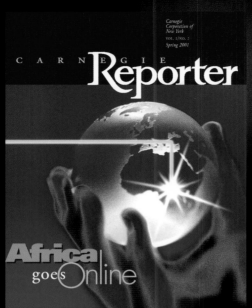

*Carnegie
Corporation of
New York*

VOL. 1/NO. 2
Spring 2001

CARNEGIE
Reporter

Africa
goes Online

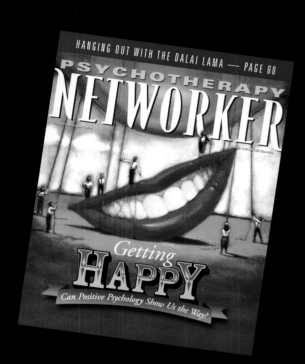

HANGING OUT WITH THE DALAI LAMA — PAGE 60

PSYCHOTHERAPY
NETWORKER

Getting
HAPPY
Can Positive Psychology Show Us the Way?

No
Way
Out

by
BILL
O'HANLON

SOMETIMES YOU JUST CAN'T DANCE AROUND THE PROBLEM

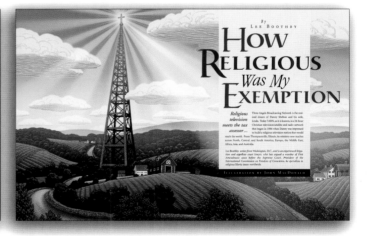

By
LEE BOOTHBY

HOW
RELIGIOUS
Was My
EXEMPTION

*Religious
television
meets the tax
assessor ...*

ILLUSTRATION BY JOHN MACDONALD

*A selection of logos for our
varied clientele. From schools
to foundations, churches to
trade associations, Dever Designs
takes pride in crafting distinctive
graphic solutions for all our
brand identity clients.*

*Opposite page: an array
of colorful reports, books and
brochures ideally suited to our
diverse clients' publishing needs.*

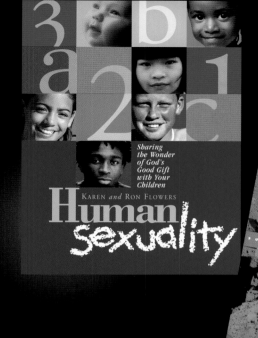

Sharing the Wonder of God's Good Gift with Your Children

KAREN *and* RON FLOWERS

Human *sexuality*

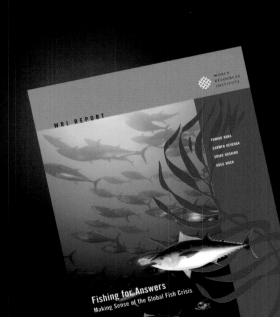

WRI REPORT

WORLD RESOURCES INSTITUTE

YUMIKO KURA
CARMEN REVENGA
ERIKO HOSHINO
GREG MOCK

Fishing for Answers
Making Sense of the Global Fish Crisis

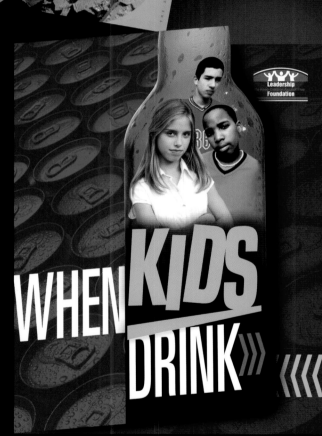

Leadership
Foundation

WHEN KIDS DRINK »

Ve Orleans

Where's the "dubyah"? Saving the world starts at home.

GLENCOE

UNDERSTANDING
Psychology

With Features Fr

GLENCOE.COM

GLENCOE

Sociology
& YOU

GLENCOE.COM

Top: A pro bono poster created for The Hurricane Poster Project, a group committed to raising awareness and funds for the victims of hurricane Katrina.

Below: Textbook covers directed at a high school audience for publisher Glencoe-McGraw Hill.

Science and art. Research and instinct. Left brain and right brain. Over the last two decades we have seen the same basic principal reworked, rewritten and even abandoned. This principal of **successful branding** is the critical collaboration of marketing objectives and creative vision. Unfortunately, these two core forces often appear to be at odds; fighting for control to ultimately declare a winner. In reality, **long term success in the marketplace** requires the two to harmonize and invest in one another. For **over 20 years DuPuis** has thrived on the rush of locking arms with the brand teams we partner with and producing **powerful results** that move the needle. Want to learn more about how our approach can help **make your brand a market leader?** Take the first step. Give us a call.

DU PUIS

877.854.8700

www.dupuisgroup.com
info@dupuisgroup.com

Los Angeles • Chicago • Germany

Unilever
Country Crock Deluxe
packaging system for a
line of side dishes

Dreyer's
Skinny Cow
brand revitalization
& packaging system

JelSert
Royal
brand revitalization
& packaging system

Kellogg's
Pop-Tarts
brand revitalization
& packaging system

Heinz
Boston Market
brand revitalization
& packaging system

Dole
Organics
packaging system for a
line of fruit products

ConAgra
Eagle Mills Flour
packaging

Dole
Wildly Nutritious
brand revitalization &
packaging system

Quaker
Crisp Bars
packaging system

Quaker
Muffin Bars
packaging system

Kellogg's
Eggo
brand revitalization &
packaging system

MasterFoods
Pedigree Butcher's Selects
packaging

MasterFoods
Uncle Ben's
Flavorful Rice
branding &
packaging system

Nestlé
Raisinets & Goobers
packaging

WD-40
Carpet Fresh
packaging

Archway
Bed & Breakfast
Crispy Classics
brand revitalization &
packaging system

Evenson Design Group
4445 Overland Avenue
Culver City, CA 90230
310.204.1995
www.evensondesign.com

Like many people who turn 30, Evenson Design Group has undergone a profound awakening, and as a result, our purpose is more clear than ever: to create inspired designs for companies seeking to sustain market value in an increasingly interdependent world.

For years, EDG has created fresh design solutions that aesthetically demonstrate balance, simplicity and efficiency–the underlying values of the emerging environmental movement. Each core value represents a different perspective in apprehending one central, universal theme: integrity. Integrity is the common denominator of all sustainable systems and graphic design is no exception. The integrity of our work comes through in our ability to develop brands and marketing campaigns which produce enduring results in the marketplace without imposing harsh enduring effects on the fragile world we share.

To that end, EDG ventures beyond switching to more efficient light bulbs and turning down thermostats; we're speaking with our clients about alternative ways of communicating their brand: sustainable ways that propel their brand and our commitment to further our own environmental awareness. Please join EDG in saving our precious resources by using minimal packaging materials, printing with earth-conscious inks and recycled papers, or even using e-announcements rather than timber. No effort is ever too small. Learn more about what you, your friends, family and workplace can do to protect the environment. Remember, we're all in this together.

UNCOMPROMISING INNOVATION
Yokohama engineers use imagination and passion to harness technology, continuously developing products with increased capability and efficiency.

UNCOMPROMISING SAFETY
Yokohama is extremely proud that its nine decades of experience and integrity have earned the absolute trust of its loyal customers.

UNCOMPROMISING PERFORMANCE
YOKOHAMA.
yokohamatire.com

UNCOMPROMISING CRAFTSMANSHIP
Every Yokohama tire is assembled with precision, skill and care, delivering the highest quality, performance and appearance.

UNCOMPROMISING HERITAGE
For over nine decades, Yokohama has used its unique approach in research and development to achieve the highest standards in performance.

UNCOMPROMISING RESULTS
Through innovation and drive, Yokohama delivers a product of uncompromising performance.

UNCOMPROMISING SPIRIT
YOKOHAMA

UNCOMPROMISING EXPERTISE
The creative engineers of Yokohama go beyond practical applications to ensure the quality and design of its products.

UNCOMPROMISING VALUES
At the heart of Yokohama lies an unwavering commitment to deliver high performance products that minimize environmental impact.

UNCOMPROMISING ACCOUNTABILITY
Company-wide activities aim to reduce CO_2 output and other wastes as Yokohama adheres to the highest principles of environmental and social responsibility.

UNCOMPROMISING COMMITMENT
YOKOHAMA

UNCOMPROMISING RESOURCEFULNESS
All new Yokohama tire products incorporate design, materials, and manufacturing technologies that work to harmonize our operations with the global environment.

1

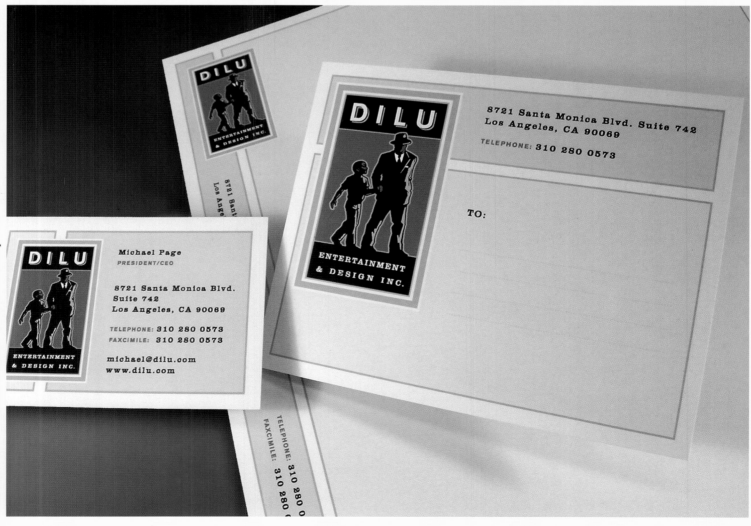

2

3

4

5

6

7

8

3. Advanced Body Work and Massage 4. Conservation Breeding Specialist Group 5. Aequitas Wealth Management 6. CoAbode 7. Floral Fruit Co. 8. MogoMedia

9

10

EDG Environmentally–Conscious Tote and Booklet

BALANCE
SIMPLICITY
EFFICIENCY

BALANCE
SIMPLICITY
EFFICIENCY

Gee + Chung Design
38 Bryant Street, Suite 100
San Francisco, CA 94105
415.543.1192
earl@geechungdesign.com
www.geechungdesign.com

Gee+Chung Design is an award-winning multidisciplinary branding firm which has developed an international reputation for designing innovative, intelligent branding strategies that help companies succeed. Led by Partners and Creative Directors Earl Gee and Fani Chung, the firm specializes in discovering what is truly unique about a company to create effective brand differentiation that clearly sets clients apart. Gee + Chung Design's powerful concept-driven solutions evoke a compelling narrative that establishes and reinforces a brand's unique voice to make a memorable connection with the audience. The firm's expertise in print, environmental and web design enables them to produce comprehensive and cohesive branding programs for enlightened companies across all media. While Gee+Chung Design has received many prestigious awards for their designs, the most rewarding aspect of their work is the consistent creation of long-term client relationships and lasting client value which enables businesses to grow and exceed their expectations.

Capabilities: Branding, Identity, Collateral, Annual Reports, Books, Packaging, Exhibits, Environmental Graphics, Websites

Clients: Apple, Adobe Systems, Applied Materials, Chronicle Books, Federal Reserve Bank, IBM, Lucasfilm, Oracle, Sony, Sun Microsystems, Symantec, Stanford University

Awards: Graphis, Communication Arts, I.D., Print, American Institute of Graphic Arts, Art Directors Club, Type Directors Club, Society of Typographic Arts, Society of Publication Designers, Society for Environmental Graphic Design

Collections: United States Library of Congress, Smithsonian Institution, AIGA Archives, Art Center College of Design Archives, San Francisco Museum of Modern Art

Education: Earl Gee: BFA with Distinction, Art Center College of Design; Fani Chung: MFA, Yale University

DCM IV Offering Memorandum

DCM is a leading Silicon Valley venture capital firm with significant technology investments in Asia and throughout the world. We branded their Offering Memorandum with a transparent plastic cover to highlight the clear difference their fund offers investors, using familiar financial symbols to identify key sections within the book.

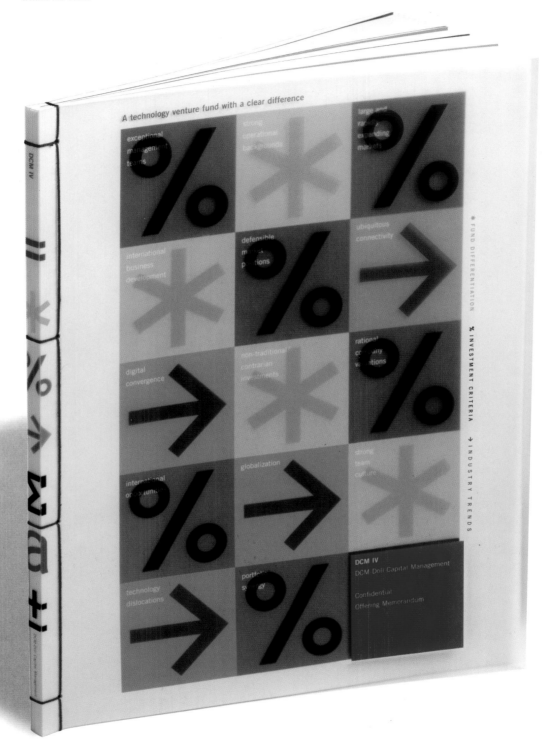

The traditional Japanese binding combined with modern materials represents the firm's careful due diligence in evaluating new technology investments. The book's impressive size and substantial presentation successfully conveyed DCM's confidence in their fund's performance, helping the fund sell out with committed investors faster than any previous fund.

DCM's holiday events are important strategic opportunities for the venture capital firm to network and build relationships with venture partners and entrepreneurs within their industry.

DCM Project READ Invitation

To connect DCM's holiday party with their support of Project READ and adult literacy, we created a Christmas tree which transforms into a tree of knowledge using books as ornaments. The die-cut from the cover becomes a holiday ornament and bookmark as a year round keepsake of the event. The party drew twice as many guests as expected and functioned as a highly successful fundraiser for Project READ.

DCM Holiday Coasters

As a departure from the traditional company holiday card, we created a set of four holiday drink coasters. The front side uses the firm's initials to create playful holiday symbols; the back side expresses the company's core values of relationships, experience, performance and opportunity for use year round. A translucent sleeve houses the coasters as a set and lists the firm's entire team. The functional and reusable gift was a distinctive, unique and memorable holiday promotion for DCM.

DCM Magic Card Invitation

A set of magic cards celebrates the Magic of the Season and announces the evening's magic show entertainment. Each card uses the magician's white gloves to spell out the firm's DCM initials while representing the Dynamic, Collaborative and Motivated attributes of the firm. A single card with all pertinent information about the party allows attendees to simply slip the card in their pocket or purse to attend the event.

DCM Passport Invitation

DCM's international scope is conveyed through our passport invitation, complete with passport stamps representing foods from distant lands, a world map of DCM's international companies and a useful list of international currencies and climates.

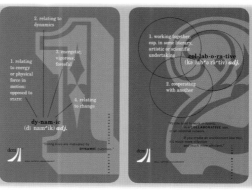

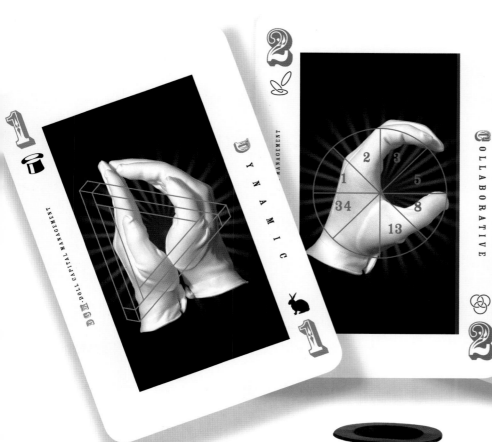

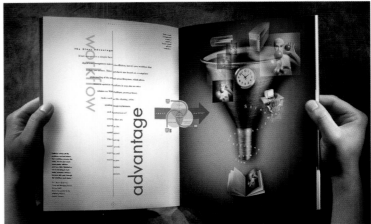

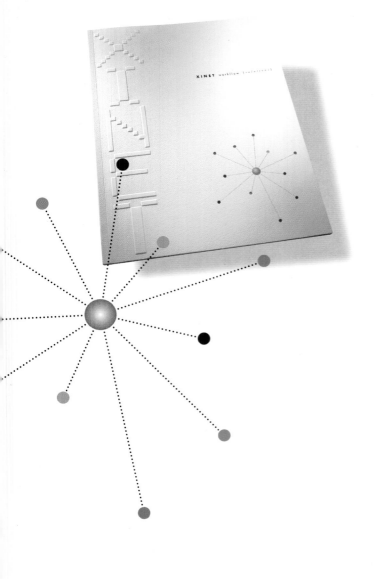

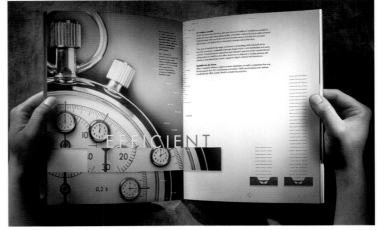

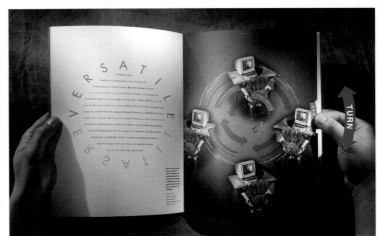

Xinet Workflow Solutions Brochure

Xinet is a developer of network server software for the printing industry. Our solution utilizes metaphors for time management, streamlined workflow and product versatility to convey key software attributes. Unusual print production techniques such as embossing, diecutting, a pull-tab and rotating wheel demonstrate Xinet's software in use in an engaging, interactive manner, enabling the brochure to function as a effective sales tool for one-on-one presentations and a memorable leave-behind for prospective customers.

Symantec Corporate Brochure

Symantec is the world's leading developer of utility software. After designing their entire packaging line, we were asked to create their product brochure. Our unusual oversize format highlights the innovative ideas behind the software Symantec develops, using the company's mission statement to frame the product features of Symantec's productivity, security and remote access software as understandable customer benefits. The mission statement creates

Qualys Tradeshow Exhibit

Qualys is the leading provider of on demand security audits to identify and protect against network vulnerabilities. At the RSA Conference, the world's largest information security technology showcase, bold security metaphors establish Qualys' "Security On Demand" theme. The reception target wall conveys the firm's focus on targeting vulner- abilities while inviting a clear view of the presentation. The giant padlock with rotating shield logo functions as a powerful symbol of information security and projects a strong presence across the hall. The keyhole entry- way opens to a calming all-white conference room for private meetings. Stools with clocks of 12 major international cities symbolize 24/7 global network security. The iconic booth was highly successful, becoming the anchor for nightly RSA Conference news coverage and generating valuable exposure for Qualys.

Qualys Tradeshow Exhibit Concepts
Three distinctly different conceptual approaches were presented to determine the most effective direction for the client.

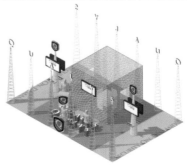

Concept 1: Overlapping Rings of Security   *Concept 2: Transparent Towers of Security*   *Concept 3: Symbolic Metaphors of Security*

GEE + CHUNG DESIGN

Gill Fishman Associates

955 Massachusetts Avenue
Cambridge, MA 02139
617.492.5666
www.gillfishmandesign.com

Recognized as one of New England's leading corporate design and branding, marketing communications and strategic design firms, Gill Fishman Associates provides expertise and consulting in launching and relaunching companies – especially high tech and biotech.

We have a passion for what we do – for the quality of our creative efforts, and for our clients and their goals.

We provide effective strategies and design to create compelling design/marketing positions which distinguish our clients from their competition.

We are committed to the growth and success of our clients.

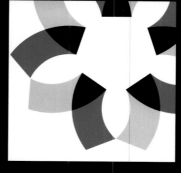

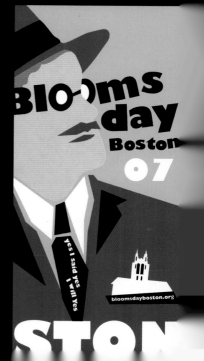

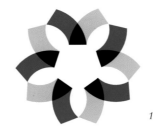

1

2

3

4

1 Spaulding Rehabilitation Hospital
2 Organic Systems
3 Black Bear Sugar Works
4 VoiceSignal

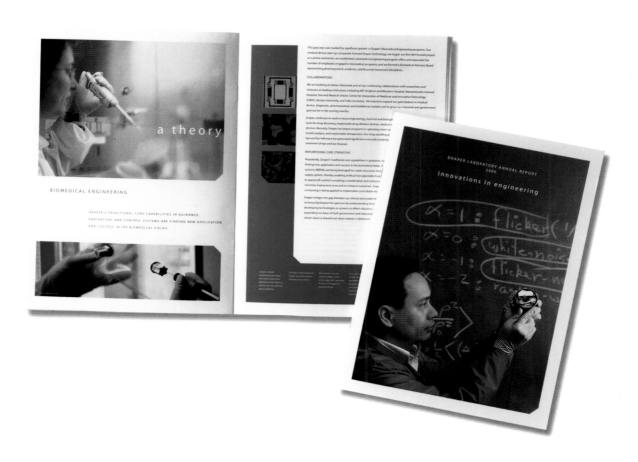

Draper Laboratory, Annual Report
Alkermes, Sales Brochure

Boys & Girls Clubs of Boston enables children who live in neighborhoods marked by poverty, crime, drug use and high teenage pregnancy rates to develop hope for the future. We help them stay safe, we guide them to say no to negative behaviors, help them dream of a better life and make plans to accomplish those dreams. Countless members ... for 114 years is life changing ... Boys & Girls Clubs of Boston has been doing they are hopeful about the f ... hope will make better choic ... report that you inspire a future.

We currently serve more th... need us. Boys & Girls Club... June 2008 is a bold but n... what our Clubs have to of... 25% over five years, and... your investment more ur...

*2004 Boston Youth Survey

47%

of BGCB member report annual hou income of under $

"

INV
IN A C
INSP
A FUTU

BOYS & GIRLS C
OF BOSTON

IMPACT

BOYS & GIRLS CLUBS OF BOSTON
ANNUAL REPORT 20 06

among

DIRECTION

YAWKEY CLUB
115 WARREN STREET
ROXBURY, MA
(617) 427-6050

From Boston, take 93 to exit 18/Ro...
Bear right onto the Mass. Ave. Ext...
Continue through 2nd traffic light...

At the 3rd traffic light (intersect...
Boston Medical Center will be on...
the road becomes Melnea Cass...
traffic light, take a left onto Ha...
(Morgan Memorial is on the le...

Follow Harrison Avenue for a...
through two sets of lights. At...
red light, Harrison Avenue and Warren...
...into the Club driveway, just...

"Without you, I would not have made it to this point. Many things that we talked about I still remember and have made the difference. I want you to know that what you do for me and other kids cannot be put into words or given a price tag. You helped to literally save my life." — Former YSPN Client

VSPN

INNOVATION

REACHING AT-RISK YOUTH AT THE CROSSROADS

Drugs. Gangs. Prostitution. Shootings. Stabbings. Poverty. That was the daily reality described by Jerome as he was growing up in Roxbury. At age 14, Jerome saw so many older males in his community going to jail or, as he says, "in the ground," that he felt he had no options, no future. Adults who had lost their way were everywhere he looked. Despite having a close-knit family with both parents at home, he felt overwhelmed by what he saw, and he told his mother that he didn't think he would live to see the age of 18.

His mother grew gravely concerned about the clothes he wore, the way he talked, the people he associated with, and the hours he kept. She recognized the signs of gang involvement. Determined not to lose her son, she called one of BGCB's programs, the Youth Service Providers Network, a partnership with the Boston Police Department. That call changed several lives and most likely saved one.

Jerome came home that day to find Denise, a YSPN social worker, waiting for him. Not surprisingly, Jerome was skeptical. Why would this woman, who didn't know him and wasn't from his community, care about him?

...the five years since that first meeting, Jerome has learned some important lessons: that there can be hope ...en when none is in sight, and that sometimes your true friends are not who you think they are.

...rose now jokes that she spent more time at Jerome's high school than he did, but she fought hard to win ...trust and to demonstrate that, together, they could turn his life around. "I'm honored that Jerome let me ...his life," Denise says. "I've learned at least as much from him as he has from me." Denise helped Jerome ...his GED, find a job, and cope when, at age 16, he became a father. Jerome says he knows that Denise is ...to support him - whenever he needs him.

...days, Jerome, now 19, works 8 hours a day for a program that will give him a scholarship for school ...is placement. At night, he takes a class at Bunker Hill Community College, where he is studying English. ...oys watching his daughter grow up, and looks forward to being a positive role model for her. Jerome ...Today I have a lot of focus, and I'm very motivated. I feel like I'm in the right place to face my future."

...rish youth are
...ed about being
...of violence.

The #1 reason young
people join gangs is
because they are afraid.

81% of parents
surveyed reported that
they would recommend
BGCB to a friend

Since 1996, YSPN has
served more than 8,000
youth (80% between
the ages of 13 and 21)
and families

BOYS & GIRLS CLUBS OF BOSTON
112th ANNUAL MEETING 20 06

PLEASE JOIN US
for a very special Annual Meeting to
celebrate the opening of the Yawkey Club of Roxbury

TAKE A TOUR OF THIS STATE-OF-THE-ART FACILITY -
a tangible example of how our Comprehensive Campaign is
already making a difference for Boston youth. Join us as we
honor those whose leadership, vision and generosity were
vital to the opening of a world class facility to serve the youth
of Roxbury. Don't miss this opportunity to connect with staff,
Board members and other friends who share your deep
commitment to the youth of Boston and Chelsea.

1

2

3

4

MIT Innovation Teams 1
New Center for Arts & Culture 2
Variagenics 3
Harvard University Center for Geographic Analysis 4
Left: Campaign & Branding for the Boys & Girls Clubs of Boston

1

2

3

4

1 Yankee Tek Ventures
2 Rampart Investment Management
3 Mass Software Council
4 Combined Jewish Philanthropies

Alnylam Pharmaceuticals, Annual Report
Circor International, Corporate Brochure
P8: A selection of not-for-profit design

miami
PH 954 739 7430
FX 954 739 3746

new york
PH 212 244 7430
FX 212 937 3613

world-wide
INFO@GOUTHIER.COM
WWW.GOUTHIER.COM

G

Who are you? Seems like a rather simple question which deserves an uncomplicated answer, for every company has a story. However, not everyone can tell it. At Gouthier Design, we position ourselves in the intellect, while we search for meaning in the art of communication. The resulting discovery not only creates a brand that is authentic to an organization, but provides an experience in the process that is extraordinary. Our story? It can be simply told: To know truth. To love beauty. To desire the good. To do the best.

Pickwick Challenge _ offshore power boating competition

Erin London _ women's apparel company

Cypress _ interior design company

Le Recherché _ purveyor of fine weddings

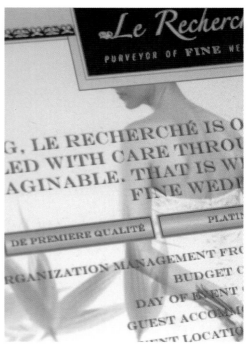

Desirability _ marriage and intimacy coaching

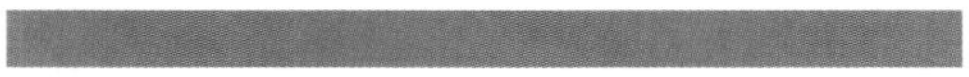

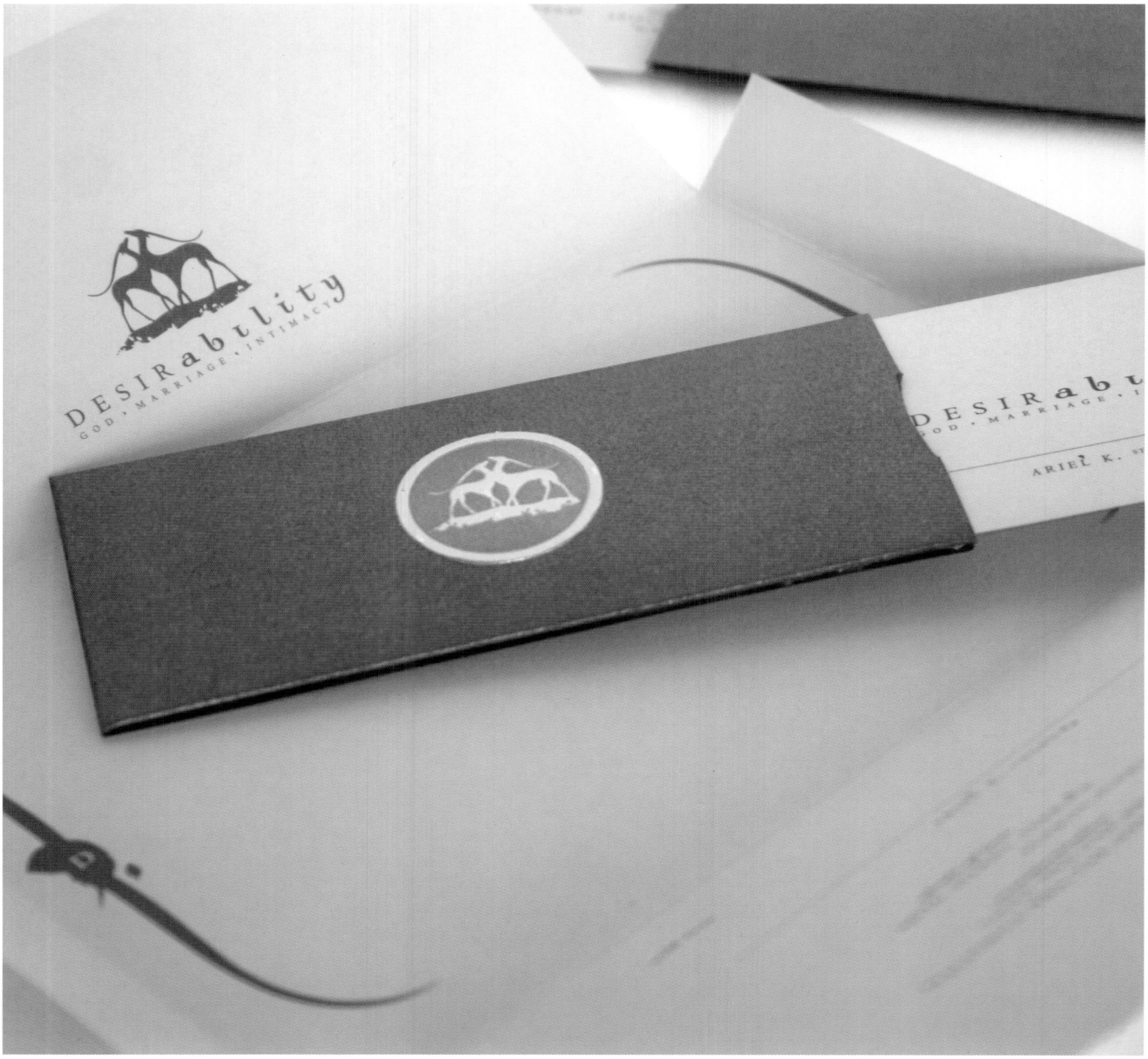

Kolter Communities _ tuscan-inspired luxury property

CHRISTIAN ART & DESIGN
ASSOCIATION

(from left to right) top row: True Engineering & Architecture, Inc., Florida's Foreclosure Alternative, LLC, Fellowship Productions; middle row: Focus Holdings, Christian Art & Design Association (CADA), Community Christian School; bottom row: Desirability, Focus Foundation, Band of Writers.

Group 22, Inc.
1205 East Grand Avenue
El Segundo, CA 90245
310.322.2210
www.group22.com

Branding. Making a unique "mark." It's a method that has been around since the Middle Ages to earmark stock animals to a specific owner. It evolved further in the 19th century when factories would literally brand their logo or insignia on the barrels they used to ship their goods. Some of the first companies to do so were Campbell Soup Company, Aunt Jemima and Quaker Oats Company in the hope of increasing consumer's familiarity with their products.

It wasn't until the 1940's that manufacturers began to realize that consumers were developing relationships with their brands in an intellectual, emotional or aesthetic sense. Now branding has grown to the point that no company can ignore the importance of having a symbolic embodiment of all the information connected to them. The logo, fonts, color schemes and symbols they employ represent in a very real sense the personality of that company.

Creating effective branding that communicates that message is our job as designers. Most clients have a strong idea of what their company is without knowing how to bring that idea across. Our clients come to us so that we can use our talent to beef up their image.

Through the years we've grown to a sizeable studio that has over thirty years of experience in the design field. From traditional print media to online and interactive work, we reckon we're ready for most any project. Our winning combination of vibrant creative energy and years of experience produces a unique personality found in few design firms.

That personality makes its mark in the passion and pride we take in our work and our studio. In turn, our clients benefit from personal attention, their own investment in the development of their identity and, most of all, branding that is as personal as it is effective.

In the end, the objective of great branding is to leave a permanent mark in the minds of the consumer. If our clients don't stand out from the rest of the herd, we haven't done our job.

MercuryMedia

*1 Logo and Brand Execution for Mercury Media,
a Santa Monica-based media buying agency*

JANE DOE
MEDIA BUYER
JDOE@MERCURYMEDIA.COM

520 BROADWAY, SUITE 400
SANTA MONICA, CA 90401
T (310) 451.2900
F (310) 451-9494

WWW.MERCURYMEDIA.COM

MercuryMedia

1 Logo for 200 Pier

*2 Slipcase and Binder for
200 Pier Brochure and
Various Collateral*

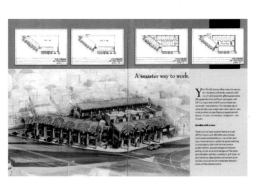

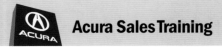
1 Logo and Brand Execution for
Acura Product Sales Training

Client: American Honda
Motor Co., Inc. and RPA

1

1 *Logo for D₂O, a Public Relations/Marketing Firm*

2 *Logo for A Sharper Home, high-end custom electronics installers*

3 *Logo for Kinsella, Weitzman, Iser, Kump & Aldisert, attornies at law*

4 *Logo for JuiceBox, personal video player*

5 *Logo for TJG Electric, private electrician*

2

3

4

5

- Background Actors
- Producers/Asst. Directors
- About Central Casting
- Press Room
- Entertainment Partners
- Store

HOT ITEM

Believe in Magic

Movie Magic's
Newest Releases
EP Budgeting 4 and
EP Scheduling 4

Available Now!

STRAIGHT OUT OF CENTRAL CASTING

Welcome to Central Casting Online, your connection to the leading background actors casting company in the United States! Central Casting has been providing the entertainment industry with background talent for more than 80 years, offering a full range of background services for every type of production from offices in Los Angeles and New York. So whether you're a producer looking for background talent, or a background actor looking for work, the crew at Central Casting has the experience and expertise to help meet all of your background needs.

- Background Actors
- Producers/Asst. Directors
- About Central Casting
- Press Room
- Entertainment Partners
- Store

HOT ITEM

Believe in Magic

Movie Magic's
Newest Releases
EP Budgeting 4 and
EP Scheduling 4

Available Now!

ACTORS   LOS ANGELES

Registration | FAQs | Registered Talents Union | Registered Talents Non-Union

Frequently Asked Payroll Questions

How soon after I work can I expect my paycheck?
Checks are due to be mailed on the Thursday after the week you worked. They may be mailed out earlier depending on when the production company turns in the complete and accurate vouchers.

Can I pick up my paycheck?
At this time, we do not have the resources for checks to be picked up. Paychecks are handled in a security area with 24 hour surveillance and delivered by our bonded driver to the post office directly. Paymasters do not have access to your paychecks.

How long does it take for me to receive my check after it's mailed?
The checks are sent first class mail. While you will receive most checks within 2 to 3 business days after they are mailed, there are times when it could take longer through the federal mail system, particularly during holiday periods.

Why do I sometimes receive my paychecks out of work date order?
Checks are not mailed out in date order. Vouchers are processed as they come in from the Production Company and Production Companies vary on how often they send in the vouchers.

I put different exemptions on my vouchers. Why don't my paychecks match the exemptions on my voucher?
We often process vouchers for more than one work date at the same time. The system will calculate all paychecks processed on any given day with the same number of exemptions from the voucher that was input into the system last. If you vary the number of exemptions you are claiming daily, we cannot guarantee that any particular voucher will match your paychecks. The box for number of dependents should reflect the amount of exemptions you are able to claim.

Do I need to write my Social Security number on my voucher each time I work?
Yes, there are many people that we payroll with the same or similar names. You will need to put your Social Security number on each voucher so we can correctly identify who we should pay. Your voucher will either be delayed or not processed if we are unable to identify who worked without this number.

THE ADVANCED CONSTRUCTION SYSTEM FOR ULTIMATE STUNTS

*1 Logo and Brand Execution
for Hot Wheels Tech Trax,
Mattel, Inc.*

680 W BEECH STREET
SUITE ONE : SAN DIEGO
CALIFORNIA 92101
PHONE : 619.234.2061
CONNECT@HOLLISBC.COM

Collaborating with clients. Connecting with audiences. Defining visual narratives. Building brands that engage. HollisBC integrates strategy and design with 20 years of business acumen to articulate a brand's soul with focus and clarity. Our equation produces meaningful results that resonate – across print, web and built environments.

Passion drives our team. Our work fuels your bottom line.

hls bc

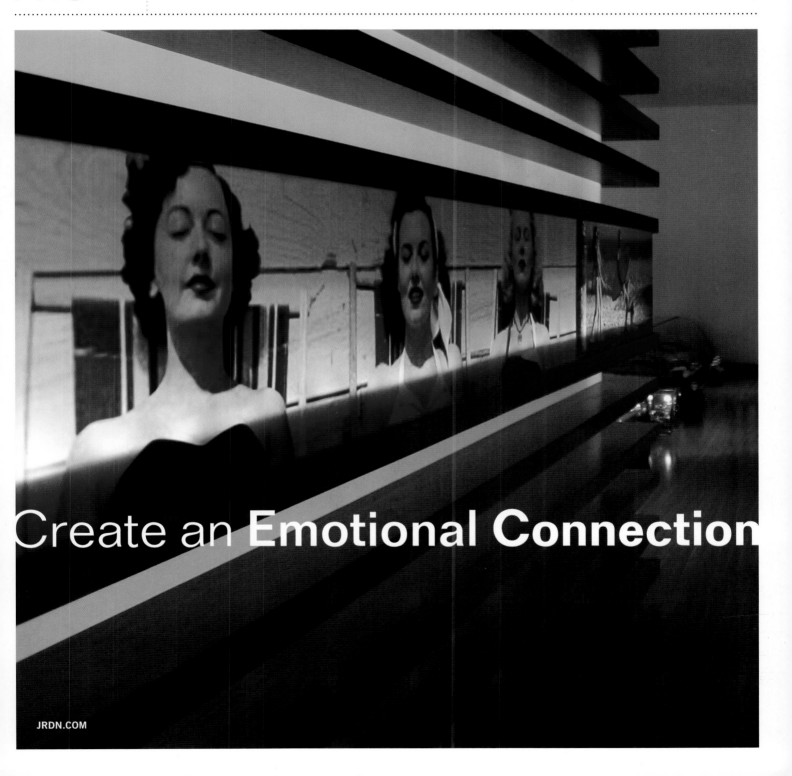

JRDN.COM

the sofia hotel

correspondence:
ONE-FIFTY WEST BROADWAY
SAN DIEGO CALIFORNIA 92101
T: 619.234.9200 ✆ F: 619.544.9879

online at:
www.thesofiahotel.com

For one nig
will rest eas

An unforgettable experience for any gue
the host. Sofia's graciousness, charm, ar
everywhere from the fine linens and soot
ambient bedside light, offering tired guest
or work from the comfort of their bed. Sof
who has thought of everything from a lap to
Her responsiveness and ability to adapt to
resonate with visitors for years to come.

This stylish boutique hotel houses 212 mod
designed to reflect a comfortable, chic feel
ences intended to invoke a sense of harmor

GUEST ROOM AMENITIES

+ All rooms and public areas are
  non-smoking
+ Convenient work stations with
  ergonomic chairs
+ High-speed Internet available (guest
  may choose speed)
+ Relaxing armchairs and ottomans
+ 20-inch flat-screen televisions with
  remote control
+ Sharper Image Universal Docking
  station alarm clock/radio
+ Illuminating, adjustable bedside lamps
+ Fine linens with white down comforters,
  plush pillows and pillow-top mattresses

+ Updated, m
  sparkling, cc
  vanity fixture
+ Separate van
  cosmetic min
+ Gilchrist & So
  toiletries in gu
+ In-room refres
  coffeemaker, n
+ Hair dryers and
+ Electronic in-ro
+ Pet-friendly roo
+ A selection of in
  services availab

THE SOFIA HOTEL
POSITIONING, IDENTITY, PR KIT, SIGNAGE, AD CAMPAIGN,
GUEST EXPERIENCE ITEMS, WEBSITE (THESOFIAHOTEL.COM)

BLANCA
POSITIONING, IDENTITY, PR KIT, SIGNAGE,
AD CAMPAIGN, WEBSITE (DINEBLANCA.COM)

LOVE CULTURE
POSITIONING, IDENTITY, CORPORATE LEASING PROGRAM,
IN-STORE COLLATERAL, RETAIL SIGNAGE PROGRAM, FIXTURE GRAPHICS

GEORGES CALIFORNIA MODERN
IDENTITY, MENU SYSTEM, SIGNAGE

DINEBLANCA.COM
SOPHISTICATED FINE DINING MEETS
MODERN LOUNGE IN THE DIGITAL
REALM. INCLUDES CLIENT CONTENT
MANAGEMENT SYSTEM (CMS).

KMA-AE.COM
TEAM RECRUITMENT, PR AND
BUSINESS DEVELOPMENT SITE FOR
A PREMIER ARCHITECTURAL FIRM.
INCLUDES CLIENT CMS.

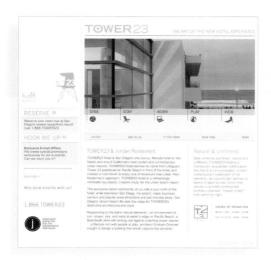

T23HOTEL.COM
ROBUST ONLINE BRAND
EXTENSION DEFINES THE ART OF
THE NEW HOTEL EXPERIENCE.

VAGABONDKITCHEN.COM
TRAVEL INSPIRED RESTAURANT
WITH A JOURNAL STYLE INTERFACE.
INCLUDES CMS TOOLS.

THESOFIAHOTEL.COM
COSMOPOLITAN HOTEL WEBSITE
THAT CAPTURES THE CORE BRAND
STRATEGY; MODERN CHARM.

HARD ROCK HOTEL:
TWO-STORY GRAND STAIR ART INSTALLATION

Hornall Anderson is a dynamic, innovative team, focused on creating unique connections with customers, constituents and communities to deliver targeted, strategic and effective branded and interactive design.

Our clients have come to expect great work based on our best-of-class beliefs. Our work is Thoughtful, and there is a reason and purpose for all we do. It contains a Creative Spark that generates an emotional response, and has a Refined Elegance through focused attention to detail. Our passion is Design.

Packaging and gift cards for Salt Lake City, UT-based O.C. Tanner's thanks.com program, offering innovative products and services for rewarding employees.

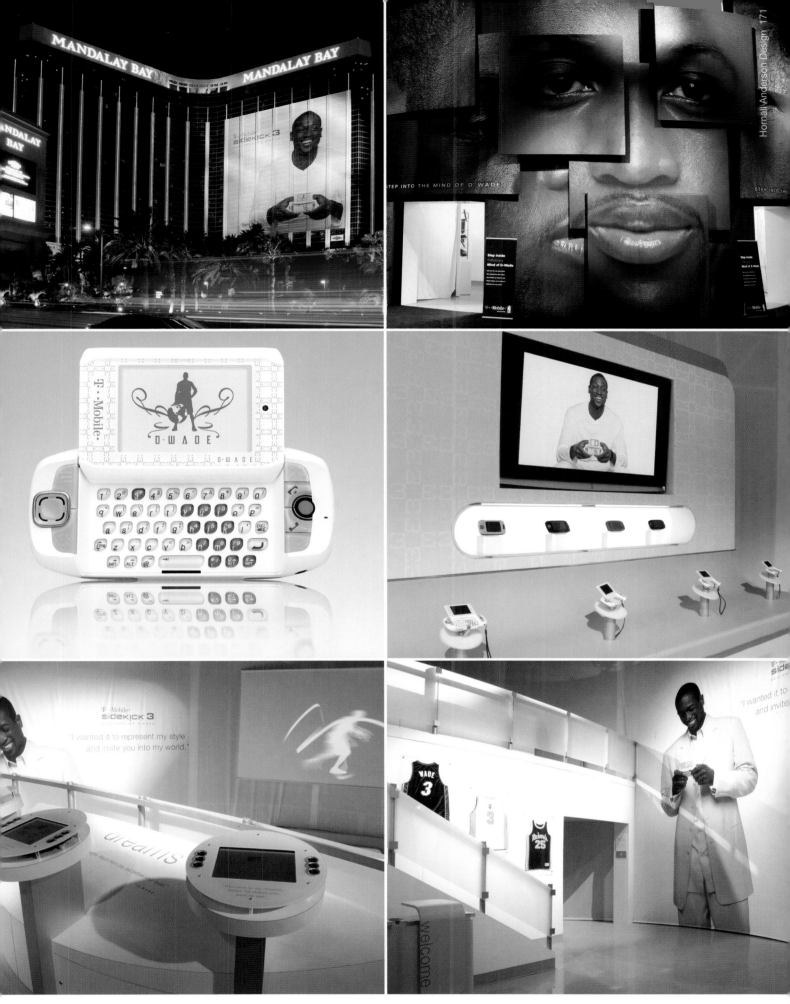

T-Mobile sponsored one of their biggest and boldest promotions at the 2007 NBA All-Star Weekend in Las Vegas for the latest Sidekick, the Dwayne Wade edition. Project scope included the creation of the world's tallest wallscape on the facade of the Mandalay Bay Hotel, an interactive environmental experience allowing fans to "Step Into The Mind of Dwayne Wade," and the limited edition mobile device.

A recruitment brochure for Seattle-based Jobster, a leading innovator of online job search communities; Schnitzer Northwest "818" brochure for a downtown Seattle professional office building; Majestic America Line brochure for a specialty cruise company providing high-end riverboat cruise experiences.

Emily's confections packaging for chocolate-covered fruit and nuts, manufactured by Tacoma-based AMES International; Windows Vista software packaging; Synergy beverage packaging for Millennium, a Beverly Hills manufacturer of nutritional drinks.

1) A Weyerhaeuser brand in panorama, ilevel.com 2) Pimp my windows with the 3M sales kiosk 3) Home finder 2.0 at redfin.com
4) Demonstrating Lotus solutions without showing product or mentioning IBM 5) Internal alignment in 30 seconds or less for TrueBlue
6) Brown is the new green with enertech.com 7) Motion design for VSP 8) Environmental interactive as an enduring brand feature for Colman Center.

9) Honoring the courage and service of those who served with memoryserves.com 10) Finding roots to understand the branches at census.ancestry.com/microsite/censuscomplete.aspx 11) From HAI with joy 12) Extending the view at 500 feet with Space Needle SkyQ 13) Learning about Weyerhaeuser's new brand iLevel with Sasquatch and friends 14) One stop branding assets on the T-Mobile Brand Portal 15) Build a smart truck with internationaltrucks.com

Majestic America Line, a specialty river-boat cruise company; Space Needle SkyQ, extending the view with interactive environmental; BLRB Architects; Schnitzer Northwest 818 office building; Blisscotti, a unique gourmet dessert; Redfin, online real estate; WetPaint, wiki-sphere for focused interests; Seattle Seahawks 12, a brand for the fans on the field; EIE, entrepreneurs and innovators for the environment; Tea Escapes, tea lozenges; iLevel, a service of Weyerhaeuser; UrbanVisions, a progressive real estate development company committed to smart growth.

IMAGE: Global Vision

2525 Main Street, Suite 204
Santa Monica, CA 90405
+ 1 310 998 8898

www.imageglobalvision.com

20TH Floor/ Central Tower
28 Queens Road Central
Hong Kong
+ 852 2159 9121

REGINA RUBINO is an award winning designer with more than 20 years experience whose focus has shifted back to the US after spending a decade in Asia and she brings a uniquely global understanding to her local perspective.

IMAGE: Global Vision Limited is a Hong Kong based corporation founded in 1997 as an entrepreneurial-focussed enterprise specializing in concept development, organization and management of "Turn-Key" operations created on behalf of leading international investors and businesses. A Los Angeles based LLC was added to service the domestic projects focussing on strategic design and branding projects.

IMAGE: Global Vision is also the expression of Regina Rubino's creative perspective and passion and respect for the word, its people, places and products. She brings a distinctive vision and connection for solving complex communication challenges on time and within budget, with sensitivity and delight.

Regina Rubino founded Louey/Rubino Design Group with Robert Louey in 1984 which has had the honor to win over 300 communication arts awards for its work around the world.

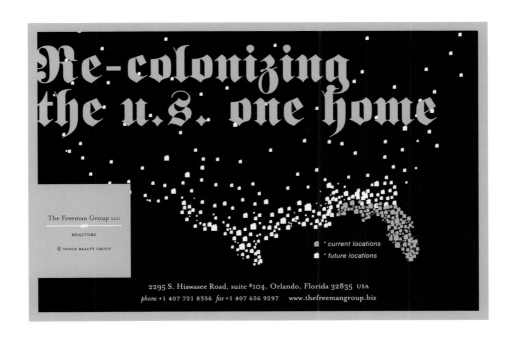

elements

BELLA CASITA

DEVELOPMENT, LLC

On Golden Pond

ENVIRONMENTAL CREATIONS

PLATEAU

SUN BLOX

REHOBOTH

DEVELOPMENT | CONSULTING

SKYLOFTS

AT MGM GRAND

NINETEEN

SEPIA

THE PENTHOUSE

NINETEEN 12

HUNTLEY

SANTA MONICA BEACH

BLUEDUCK
TAVERN

PARK HYATT

PARIS

VENDÔME

The Beverly Hills

REGINA RUBINO
{1} 310 871 8789

REGINA RUBINO
{1} 310 871 8789

roberto @robertoblandin.com
BLANDIN
M 1·310·779·8789 F 1·310·827·8828

· INSTRUMENTS ·
GUITAR (6 & 12 string Acoustic & Electric), BASS,
CUATRO (Venezuelan), TRES (Cuban), CHARANGO (Bolivian),
MANDOLIN, CAVAQUINHO (Brazilian), TIPLE (Colombian), VOCALS

kor group
374 Congress Street
Boston, MA 02210
617.330.1007 tel
617.330.1004 fax
www.kor.com

kor group is a visual communications firm that builds successful brands and keeps them moving in the online and offline world.

Think

We believe that communications challenges are more than problems to be solved — they're unique opportunities to uncover new insights about an organization. Our work focuses on uncovering the ideas and beliefs most integral to an institution. We get to the most important part — the core.

Create

Our creative process revolves around a deep respect for our clients' knowledge. Working closely together we gather information and gain awareness that allows us to repeatedly focus and refine our efforts. The result is a logical project plan, a clear creative vision, and a final project that exceeds expectations and produces results.

Share

We build effective, memorable brands that engage our clients's intended audience. Brands that are honest, authentic, and true. In a world as ephemeral as design, it is our commitment to big picture results and long-term goals that distinguishes us — and truly defines us.

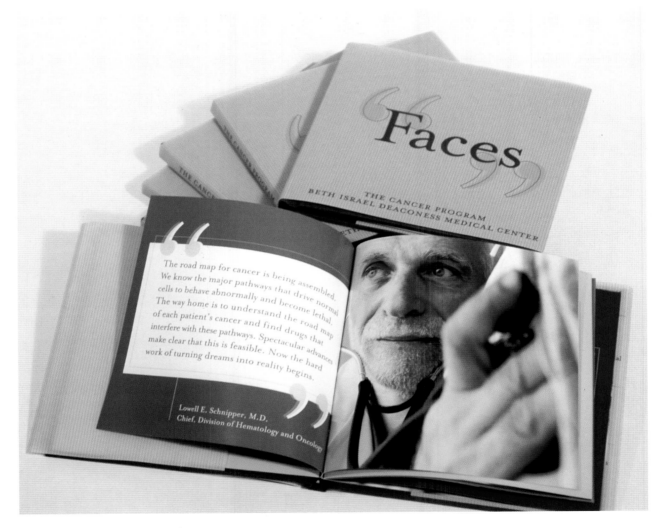

ADVENTURES IN EMERGING TECHNOLOGIES

VIRTUAL WORLDS
AND DIGITAL DOMAINS

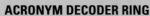

IMAGINE THE POSSIBILITIES

COMMUNITY GATHERING,
client: Cal-Sportbike

BUILD A **COMMUNITY**

I KNOW I CAN WIN THIS RACE

ENTERTAIN AND ENGAGE

VISUALIZE CONCEPTS.
GAUGE CONSUMER REACTION
IN A NEW CONSUMER TESTING
ENVIRONMENT

BUILD AND SUPPORT A
FAN BASE WITH
EVENTS AND
ENVRONMENTS

Project created for Ferrari

SUPPORT TRADITIONAL
ADVERTISING AND WEB
PRESENCE

VIRTUAL DOG PARK,
client: dogpark.com

REINFORCE **BRAND
MESSAGING** AND
PRODUCT BENEFITS

WOW THIS HAS A LINK TO THE WEB SITE

VIRTUAL SHOWROOM,
client: Cal-Sportbike

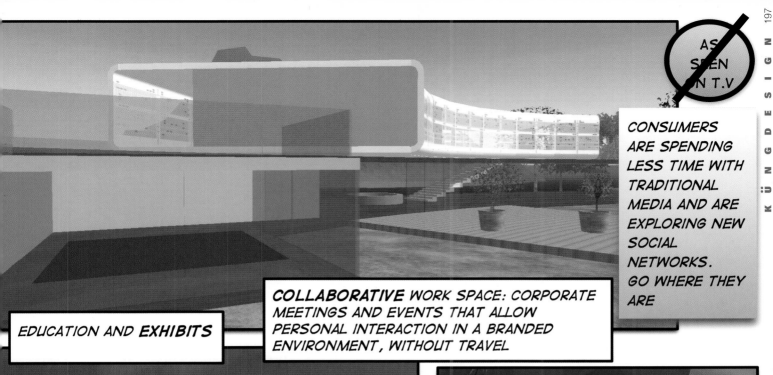

CONSUMERS ARE SPENDING LESS TIME WITH TRADITIONAL MEDIA AND ARE EXPLORING NEW SOCIAL NETWORKS. GO WHERE THEY ARE

EDUCATION AND **EXHIBITS**

COLLABORATIVE WORK SPACE: CORPORATE MEETINGS AND EVENTS THAT ALLOW PERSONAL INTERACTION IN A BRANDED ENVIRONMENT, WITHOUT TRAVEL

ENGAGE IN **CONVERSATION** WITH CONSUMERS

I AM GOING TO ORDER THOSE BRAKE CABLES

I JUST TESTED THOSE AND...

EXPLORE COLLABORATIONS AND NEW OPPORTUNITIES TO CONNECT WITH CONSUMERS

INTRODUCE PRODUCT AND SERVICES IN A 3-DIMENSIONAL **E-COMMERCE** ENVIRONMENT

VIDEO INTEGRATION ENABLES **STORYTELLING**, EXTENDS USE OF ADVERTISING AND PROMOTIONAL MEDIA

WE DON'T LIMIT OURSELVES TO VIRTUAL WORLDS - WE UTILIZE PLENTY OF VISUALIZATION TOOLS

3-D MODELS PRESENTED IN A WEB INTERFACE ALLOW CONSUMERS TO INTERACT WITH NEW PRODUCTS, GAINING **CUSTOMER** REACTION AND **INSIGHT** BEFORE A BRAND GOES TO MARKET

3-D DESIGN, MODELING AND RENDERING ENABLES CONCEPTS TO BE VISUALIZED BY CLIENT TEAMS AND RETAIL PARTNERS - BEFORE THEY'RE BUILT

client: The Wine Group

client: Underdog Wine Merchants

client: F'Real Foods

VIDEO ON DEMAND DELIVERS A CUSTOM-CREATED MESSAGE OR **EXTENDS THE REACH** OF ADVERTISING CAMPAIGNS TO WEB SITE VISITORS.

client: Franzia Winery

OUR 3-D VISUALIZATION WORK IS ANCHORED BY OUR EXPERIENCE IN BRANDING, STRATEGY, WEB, GRAPHIC AND ENVIRONMENTAL DESIGN. A FULL-SERVICE CREATIVE STUDIO, OUR PORTFOLIO REPRESENTS WORK ACROSS DISCIPLINES, BORDERS AND TECHNOLOGIES.

RETAIL STORE CHAIN, INTERIOR AND SIGNAGE DESIGN

client: Arsoa, Japan

BRANDED APPAREL

client: Kasikorn Bank Public Company Limited, formerly Thai Farmers Bank, Thailand

PACKAGING DESIGN

client: Underdog Wine Merchants

WEB SITE DESIGN, VIDEO

Have you Heard The News?

WATCH OUT!

This Wine Jumps Out of Your Glass!™

Now Being Poured On Board

©2006 FishEye Winery,Soledad, CA

client: FishEye Winery

Without logic, no one will be persuaded
Without magic, no one will care

Fourteen years ago we started out with three clients, boundless optimism, and the vague notion of creating a place based on our personal values and deeply motivated by meaningful, provocative design. Our goal was to introduce clients to world-class work created through an uncommonly straightforward and responsive partnership, and based on collaboration and celebration, or that intriguing combination of Logic and Magic.

Founding Principals Pam and Richard Shear each bring a lifetime of design experience in personal care, food, beverage, technology, and entertainment categories.

Today, we have more clients, more case histories, and more space in our new office on the river in historic South Norwalk. With this growth comes the strong conviction that creativity remains a collaboration. That truly successful design depends as much on engaging with a consumer as it does the brilliance of a designer, as much on the small everyday details of client service as our aesthetic values. Creativity is not just about taste. It's about optimism, and sustainability . . . and most importantly, it's about remembering that great design makes a difference in peoples' lives.

LMS Design, Inc.
15 North Water Street
South Norwalk, CT 06854
203.831.9100
www.lmsdesign.com

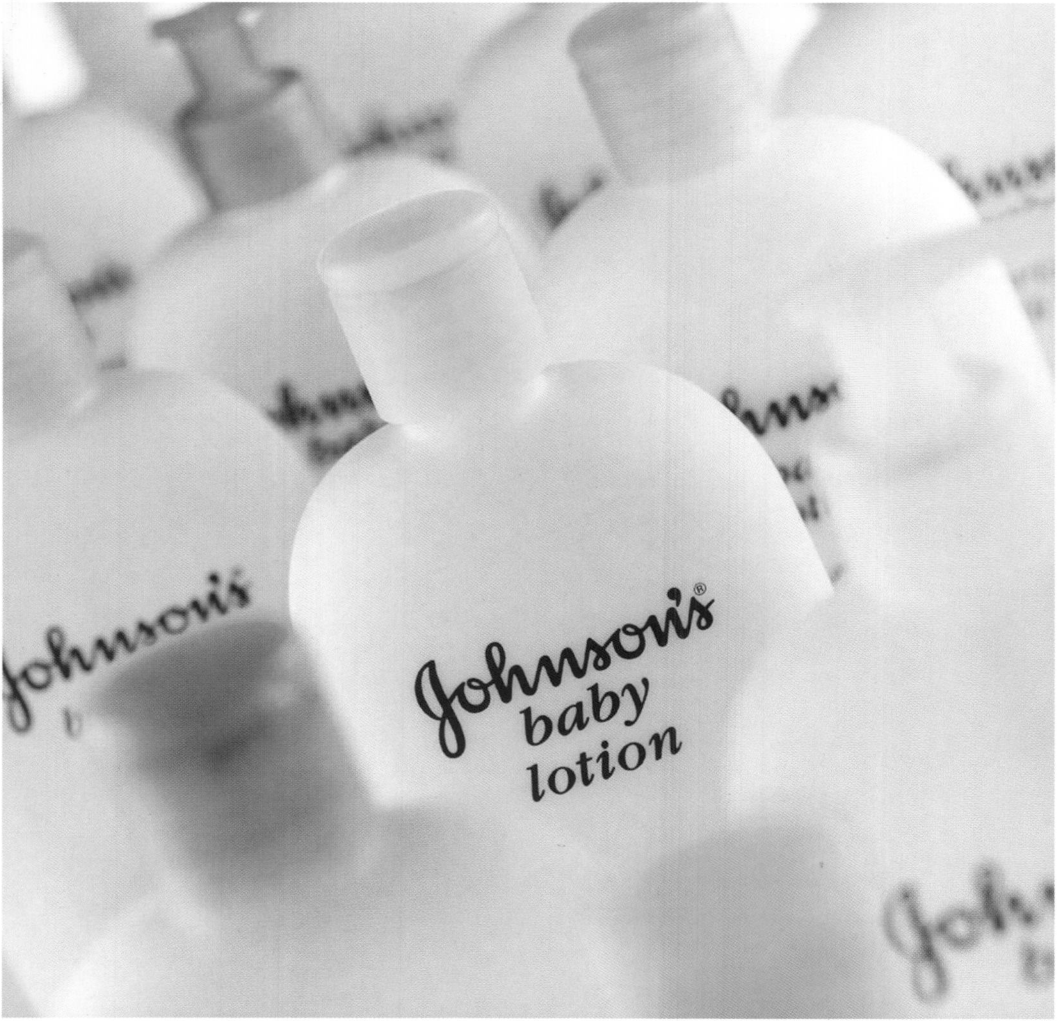
Johnson's®
baby
lotion

Global brand identity and package design program for Johnson & Johnson's baby line that brings a consistently fresh new look to all primary package materials, surfaces, color palette and graphics.

Brand and package redesign for Aveeno products, including a new look for each primary and secondary package structure, bottle design, and label graphics. The program included all recent new product development and line extensions.

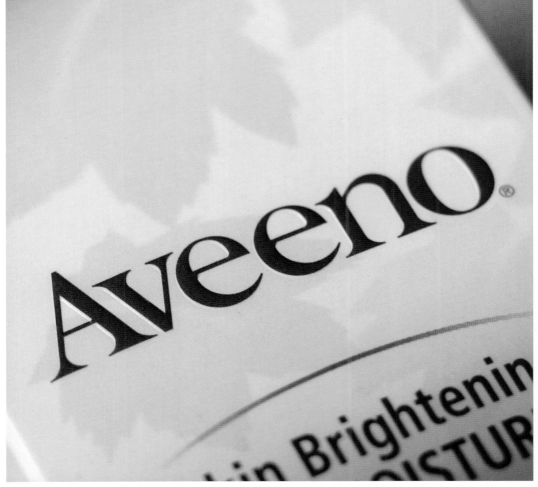

Design development for Pernod Ricard of an extensive line of Seagram's branded products, including the traditional gin and vodka as well as the specialty products Gin & Juice and Distiller's Reserve.

Brand identity and package design for clients including Duracell, Hasbro, Ahold, Gerber, and Kraft

109 Vickery Street
Roswell, GA 30075-4926
770.645.2828
www.lorencyoodesign.com
jan@lorencyoodesign.com

For most non-designers, "environmental graphic design" may sound like an eco-centric approach to graphic design. According to Lorenc+Yoo Design (LYD), it is a strategy for creating direction for people in public places and enhancing their sensory experience. Jan Lorenc, principal of LYD, directs a firm with 30 years of experience in architectural signage, exhibits, product design and branding, and shares his understanding of "how" and "why" environmental graphic design continues to be relevant today.

"Environmental graphics are tools that aid in visitor navigation and improve the experience," explains Lorenc. "They're functional, but they also serve as the site's architectural jewelry and enhance it; they complement the venue."

LYD's key to effective environmental graphic design lies not only in the balance between utility and an eye-pleasing aesthetic. The design must also observe contextual and historical relevance as well as the client's objective. "Our passion is to express the client's passion," Lorenc says. "Colors, materials, typography, lighting, and other details must all work together so the environment is seamless and so that the site, the building, and the interiors all look like they have been cut from the same cloth. We aim to use environments to send the right messages in useful and beautiful ways."

"Our work at the Gaylord Texan Resort is one example of how an environmental graphics campaign can compliment an overall environment," says Lorenc. "We worked diligently with the developer's team so that we could understand the materials that we needed to use, as well as the original design's thematic approach. We determined how we could design a grounded and detailed project so that the signage looked like it had been there from the very beginning."

For the Gaylord Resort in Grapevine, TX, the LYD team balanced the prairie-like atmosphere of the site with a signage program that used natural stones, earth tones and minimalist shapes. The team integrated a modern Texan theme into the design, echoing the historic western aesthetic of area while also maintaining a fresh look.

LYD's ensemble of architects, industrial designers, and graphic designers also sought to achieve seamless integration with the site for the gateway signage design for Firewheel Town Center in Garland, TX. "Custom-built lighting, ironwork and strong typography produced a strong piece that greets mall visitors immediately and makes a bold impression," Lorenc says. "It makes a statement that's both local and modern. The team engaged in the project in a way that was conscious of the site's architectural details and how the pieces could enhance those details in a sophisticated fashion, locked into the overall design scheme."

While integration by context is often relevant, contrast is another tool in the designer's arsenal. "There are times when integration is less appropriate, when the design of a sculpture or signage program should contrast. Our approach is to live and breathe the project to fully understand the design intent and how we can go with the flow of suggesting a counterpoint to what already exists," says Lorenc.

Wayfinding programs for Oakbrook Mall (Oakbrook, IL), Newport Centre Mall (Jersey City, NJ) and the Memphis Library (Memphis, TN) use contrasting color to draw visitors' eyes to useful information. "Many times, signage works well because it's noticeable. That doesn't mean that it's obnoxious or annoying, but that it informs easily and clearly," Lorenc says. "Our designs achieve a subtle contrast with the environments in which they're sited."

LYD's environmental graphic design can also include innovative sculptural elements. "In the case of our public art assignments, we look at innovative uses of materials and lighting–during both day and night conditions–and seek to make the pieces timelessly relevant," says Lorenc. The lobby directory at 3003 Perimeter Summit in Atlanta, GA features a stacked aqua-colored glass structure that builds up to a pointed pinnacle, providing a large area around its midsection where visitors can locate tenants easily.

"Environmental graphic design is versatile and varied," says Lorenc. "but good environmental graphic design is consistent in its ability to blend form and function seamlessly and elegantly. We take this approach with all of our projects, and use it to tell the client's story to achieve their goals. This is the secret formula of what we've done for nearly 30 years…and we're just getting started."

Firewheel Town Center
Garland, TX

Dadeland Mall
Miami, FL

Oakbrook Mall
Chicago, IL

Newport Centre Mall
Jersey City, NJ

Newport Centre Mall
Jersey City, NJ

Dadeland Mall
Miami, FL

3003 Perimeter Summit
Atlanta, GA

maddocks

inspired thinking

Maddocks is a leading design and marketing agency serving corporate clients since 1973. Over the years, we have earned a solid reputation for outstanding creative design and breakthrough communication.

Our services include strategic planning, brand identity, advertising, packaging, collateral and web design.

Highly successful campaigns for such renowned brands as Red Bull, Ketel One, Walt Disney, Procter & Gamble, Sony and Warner Brothers reflect our ability to deliver conceptual creative solutions that meet immediate needs and future expectations.

From concept to completion, Maddocks takes a comprehensive approach to corporate identity and brand development. We understand the importance of building a partnership along the way, and that attention to detail can be as important as excellence in design.

At Maddocks, we enable our clients to achieve greater success by helping them to create and manage brand value and build loyalty. The products and services we've helped launch are widely distributed and used by millions of people every day.

If you have a business to build or market to capture, call Maddocks. We look forward to serving you.

2011 pontius avenue
los angeles, california 90025
310.477.4227
www.maddocks.com

BRAND DEVELOPMENT   STRATEGY   PACKAGING   IDENTITY   NEW MEDIA

over 30 years developing unique, innovative + targeted brands

01

02

03

04

05

Platinum Equity

06

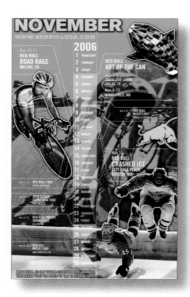
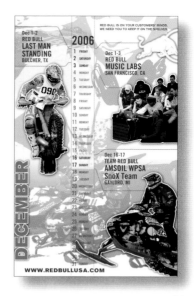

01

02

03

04

01 **Red Bull** Calendars
02 **Red Bull** 12 Can Packaging
03 **Terrazzo** Marketing Kit
04 **Terrazzo** Identity

**dog
bliss**

unleash pure joy

05

06

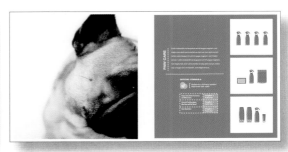

07

01

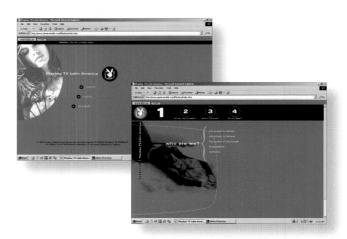

02

03

01 **Playboy Latin America** Stationery
02 **Playboy Latin America** Website
03 **Playboy Latin America** Brochure

04 Relastin Identity
05 Relastin Packaging
06 Pelican Packaging

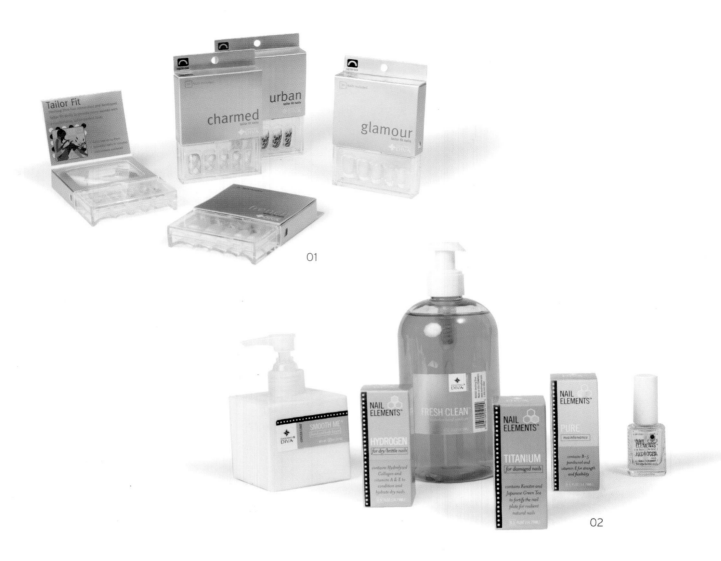

01

02

03

04

391-393 Eddy Street
Providence, RI 02903
401.331.2891
www.mgrear.com

Visual identity is the "face" an organization shows the public; wide exposure secures its position as one of the single most important aspects of a company's projected image.

A successful identity is unique, gestalt-like, uncomplicated (so as to remain memorable) and active. It is critical that the identity be versatile: maintaining its integrity when used in all media outlets.

A well conveyed identity does not exhaust its meaning quickly, it is both profound and as timeless as possible.

Malcolm Grear Designers has an extensive portfolio of successful visual identity and branding programs that have brought strength, consistency, distinction and improved performance to organizations worldwide.

Malcolm Grear Designers is a full service design firm.

Identity/Branding

Print/Publications

Interactive/Web

Signs/Wayfinding

Exhibition Design

Place/Recognition

Packaging/Trade Shows

Dyax

"Every organization has an identity, if not by plan, then by default."

MALCOLM GREAR

Dyax Corp
Identity/Branding/Signs
An innovator in biopharmaceuticals.

Lifespan
Identity/Branding/Signs/Graphics Standards
A healthcare network.
Right: Print materials produced by Lifespan
following branding guidelines.

PharmaCare
Identity/Branding
A leading prescription benefit manager
which bridges the gap between
the pharmaceutical industry and the
healthcare system.

Elixir Pharmaceuticals
Identity/Branding/Signs
A biopharmaceutical company
focused on testing and preventing
age-related diseases.

Rhode Island Department of Health
Identity/Branding/
Graphics Standards Website
A state agency protecting and
promoting the health and safety of
the people of Rhode Island.

Foster Gallery
Noble and Greenough School
Identity/Branding/Publications/
Website/Signs

G F A O L S T E E R R Y

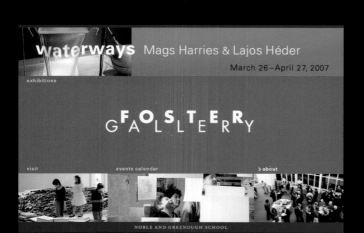

The Institute of Contemporary Art/Boston
Signs/Wayfinding/Donor Recognition
The ICA's new building, by architects Diller
Scofidio + Renfro, is the first new museum to
be built in Boston in nearly 100 years.

National Building Museum
Exhibition: *David Macaulay: The Art of Drawing Architecture*

Identity/Exhibition Design/Publications
The exhibition explores the fascinating creative process of world-renowned author and illustrator, David Macaulay.

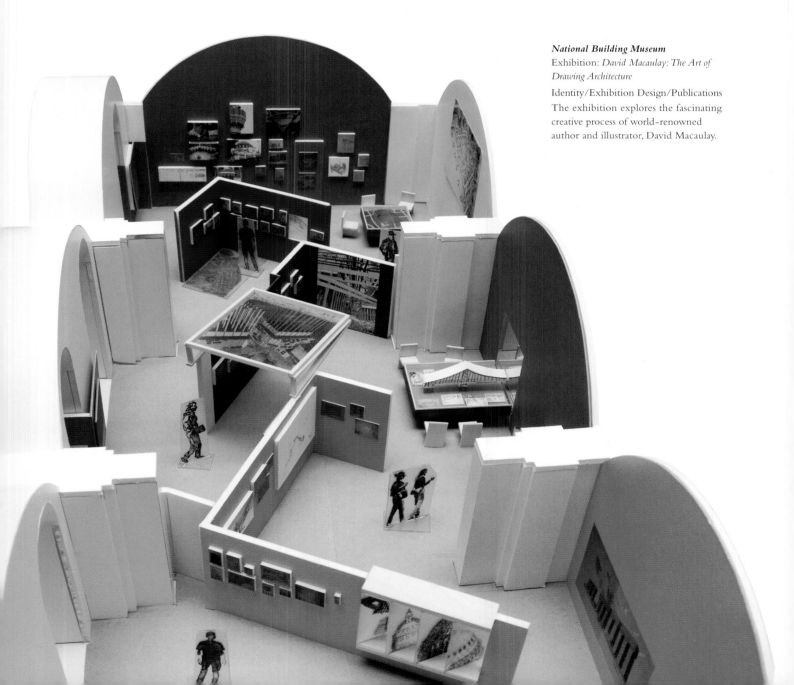

International Institute
Rhode Island

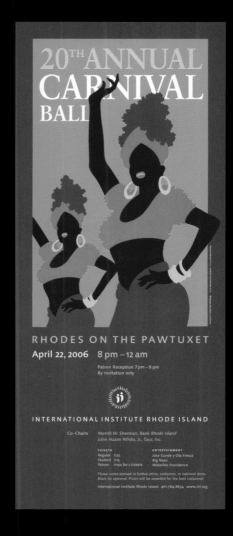

Carnival Ball posters, in collaboration with
illustrator Chris Van Allsburg.

International Institute of Rhode Island
Identity/Branding/Publications/Signs
An organization that provides educational, legal and
social services to immigrants and refugees throughout
Rhode Island and southeastern Massachusetts.

Nine-foot banners with illustrations by IIRI Students.

WEINBERG
GLASS

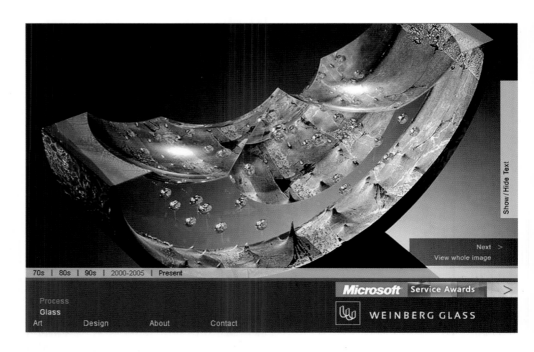

Weinberg Glass
Identity/Website
Steven Weinberg, glass artist.

**Microsoft Corporation
and Weinberg Glass**
Microsoft Service Awards Website

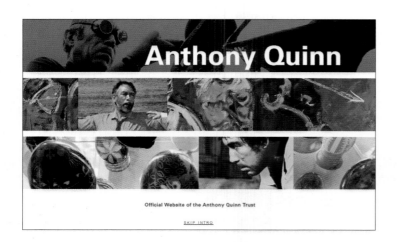

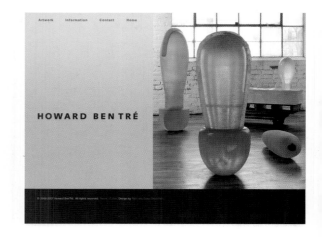

Anthony Quinn Foundation
Branding/Website

Howard Ben Tré, Artist
Website

Brown University
Signs/Wayfinding
Urban campus construction
fence wrap and wayfinding system

We build brands for packaging. The work presented on these pages has been created for a wide range of clients, small and large. Each project presented singular challenges.

Accordingly, the design solution for each project took different forms. A different style or appearance was fashioned which was the correct one for the demands of its particular marketplace.

It is to be expected then that we do not have a "style" or look that typifies our work.

What is a constant, however, is our guiding belief that every company, every brand, every product has at its core certain key traits that it and it alone possesses.

Our job is to discover and breathe life into a brand so that it will have depth and color and character and a persona—almost lifelike human qualities—with which every consumer can connect emotionally.

But one more thing is absolutely essential: It must sell. And good design sells.

Branding

Packaging

Trademarks

Marketing

Environmental Design

Collateral

1984 Old Mission Drive
Suite A15
Solvang, CA 93463
805.686.5166
www.markoliverinc.com

Tribe™

MATSUMOTO INCORPORATED

127 WEST 26TH STREET, NEW YORK, NY 10001

212.807.0248

MATSUMOTOINC.COM

Matsumoto Incorporated (est. 1987) is a design consulting firm based in New York City specializing in brand identity, packaging, advertising, website design, and publication design. Principal and President Takaaki Matsumoto, a native of Japan who moved to the United States in 1974, and his staff service a broad range of national and international clients. Matsumoto Incorporated counts among its clients Art Center College of Design; The Fabric Workshop and Museum; Maharam; The Metropolitan Museum of Art; Museum of Contemporary Art, Chicago; Museum of Modern Art; Philadelphia Museum of Art; Steuben; Simon and Schuster; and the Solomon R. Guggenheim Museum. Its international clients include Comme des Garçons and Sazaby, Inc. Matsumoto Incorporated has been recognized with numerous honors and design awards and has work included in the collections of various museums, including the Library of Congress, The Chicago Athenaeum (Museum of Architecture and Design), The Montreal Museum of Decorative Arts, Image for Peace (Montreal), the Cooper-Hewitt National Design Museum, and The Berman Collection.

● Art Center College of Design

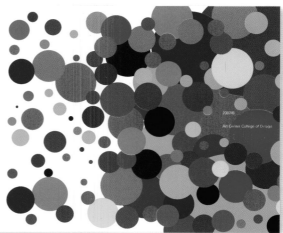

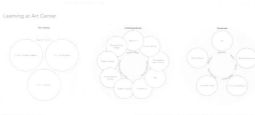

Learning at Art Center

Meeting New Challenges

A Leader in Art and Design Education

A History of Art and Design Leadership

Designing the Future

Undergraduate and Graduate Programs

About this catalog

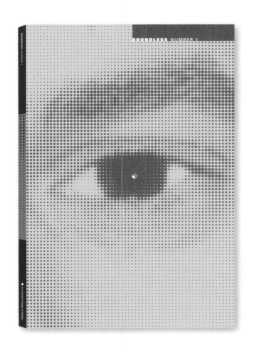
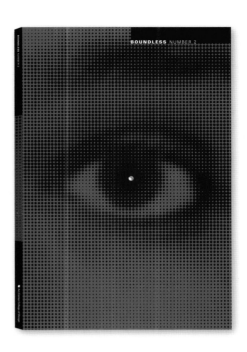

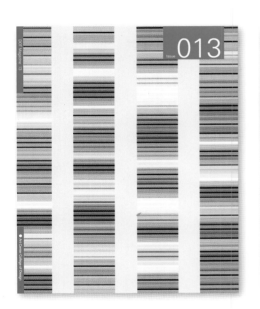

Art Center College of Design (top to bottom): *Boundless*, a series of publications featuring interviews with prominent alumni | *DOT*, semiannual magazine | 2004 & 2006 biannual design conference, identity and collateral

|maharam|

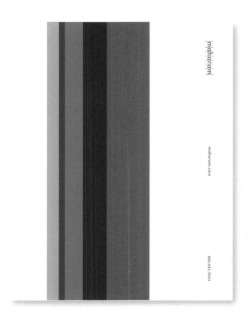  

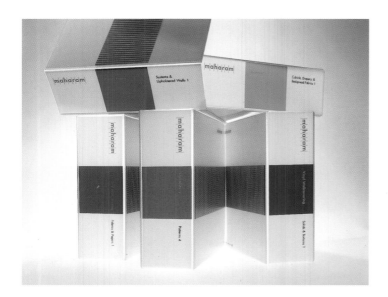 

Maharam: Logo | Advertisement series | Binder system | Stationery system
Perfumes Isabell (right): Package design

NEW MATERIAL AS NEW MEDIA: THE FABRIC WORKSHOP AND MUSEUM

BY MARION BOULTON STROUD

Doug Aitken

American, born 1968, lives in Los Angeles

Born in Redondo Beach, California, Doug Aitken received his BFA from the Art Center College of Design in Pasadena in 1991. In the 1990s Aitken became known for his video installations, which involve a productive cross-pollination of styles borrowed from television advertising, Hollywood cinema, experimental and documentary film, as well as the music video genre—a blend he refers to as "pure communication." Aitken was awarded the International Prize at the Venice Biennale in 1999, and the Larry Aldrich Foundation Award in 2000. His work has appeared in solo exhibitions at venues such as the Centre Georges Pompidou, Paris (2002); the Serpentine Gallery, London (2001); and the Museum of Contemporary Art in Los Angeles (2000). Major group shows include Let's Entertain organized by the Walker Art Center, Minneapolis, (2000); the Biennale of Sydney 2000 (Museum of Contemporary Art, Sydney); and the 1997 and 2000 Whitney Biennials (Whitney Museum of American Art, New York).

Doug Aitken's collaborative project with The Fabric Workshop and Museum (FW+M), *Interiors*, comprises a series of filmic narratives projected onto an architectural fabric structure. Shot in locations around the world, the constituent narratives initially appear to be unrelated. One sequence depicts a businessman in a Tokyo penthouse at sunset talking to himself, another portrays an African American man wandering around a bombed out neighborhood in Los Angeles. As the viewer moves through the installation, the rhythms in the sound element of each narrative grow increasingly synchronized. Eventually, the sound components of each join into one rhythm, growing faster and faster into a moment of complete visual and audible transformation. The moment passes, and the sound for each segment falls back into its own disparate, random rhythm, but the individual stories are each affected and changed by the temporary alignment. *Interiors* offers flashing moments of order in an ever-changing world.

Each of these narratives is fictional, and carefully scripted and arranged by Aitken. For example, the man in the Tokyo penthouse is actually an auctioneer from the Tokyo fish market; the African American man is in reality a member of the hip-hop duo, Outkast; another segment takes place in a vast, symmetrical helicopter factory and shows a performance choreographed by a professional dancer. These rich, saturated environments are vividly portrayed in the striking imagery for which the artist is known.

While at the FW+M, Aitken experimented with a wide array of reflective, transparent, and opaque materials, which were stretched onto a variety of architectural forms. These fabric-covered shapes were used in the filming of the piece to achieve special visual and lighting effects; they are also a part of the final installation, serving as the scrims onto which the videos are projected. These sculptural experiments allowed the artist to continue his ongoing conceptual explorations while breaking out of conventional narrative structure and the bounded two-dimensional frame. Moving through the physical installation, visitors actively participate in the poetic construction of various themes that run through this work, including ideas about mapping, navigation, and placing oneself in new realities.

Interiors, 2002. Production images. Dimensions vary with installation.

Interiors, 2002 (this page and facing page). Production images. Dimensions vary with installation.

Conceptual sketch for development of warped elements, 2002 (following pages). Composite digital rendering.

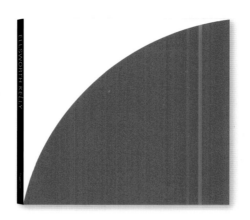

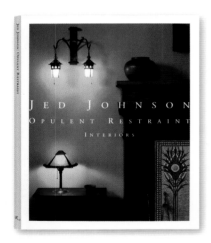

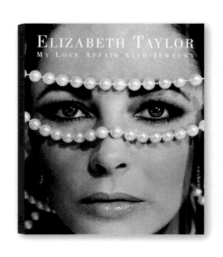

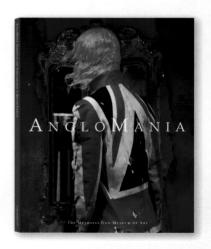

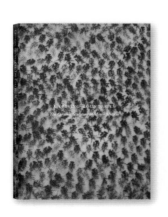

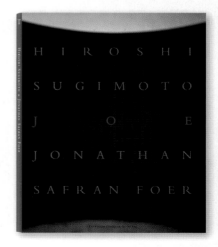

Publications (left to right, top to bottom): *Robert Mapplethorpe And The Classical Tradition: Photographs and Mannerist Prints | Ellsworth Kelly | Roy Lichtenstein | Alex Katz: Small Paintings | Wild: Fashion Untamed | Francesco Clemente: Retrospective | Jed Johnson: Opulent Restraint Interiors | Elizabeth Taylor: My Love Affair With Jewelry | AngloMania: Transgression and Transformation in British Fashion | Hiroshi Sugimoto | Crossing Boundaries: The Ceramic Sculpture of Mineo Mizuno | Joe*

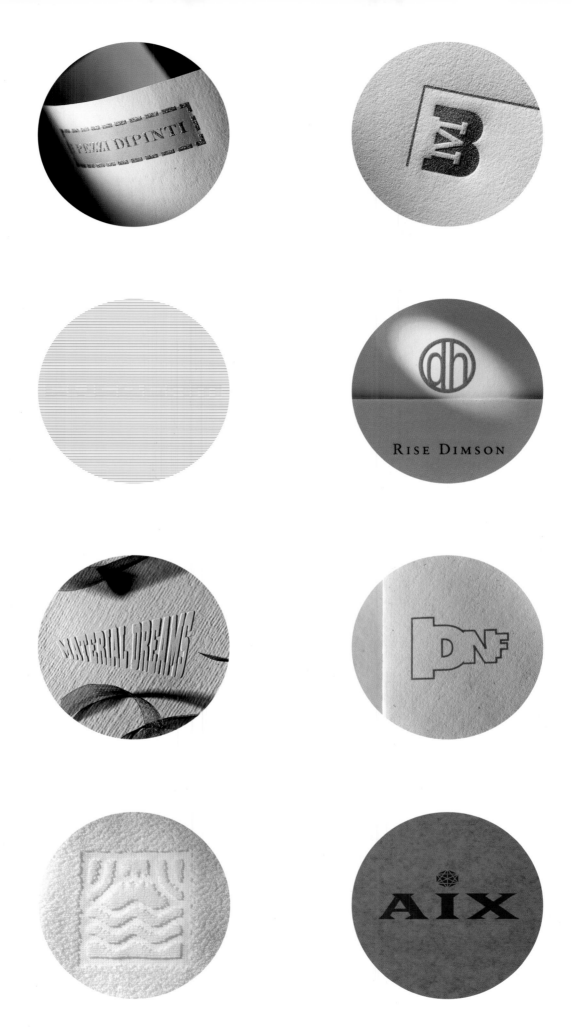

Logo Designs (left to right, top to bottom): I Pezzi Dipinti | Merill C. Berman Collection | Eyebeam | Dimson Homma | Material Dreams | International Design Network Foundation | Awashima Hotel | Sazaby AIX

McElveney & Palozzi Design Group, Inc.

McElveney & Palozzi Design Group, Inc.

1255 University Avenue
Suite 200
Rochester, NY 14607
Phone: 585-473-7630
www.mandpdesign.com

McElveney & Palozzi Design Group is a team of business strategists, creative problem solvers, visual explorers, and production specialists all focused on our clients' goals. From corporate and consumer brand building to small business marketing, McElveney & Palozzi has achieved results in the areas of identity and branding, print collateral, advertising design, packaging, and web/emerging media for over 25 years. Each unique and successful branding solution truly inspires and effectively communicates.

A Full-Service Marketing Communications and Design Firm

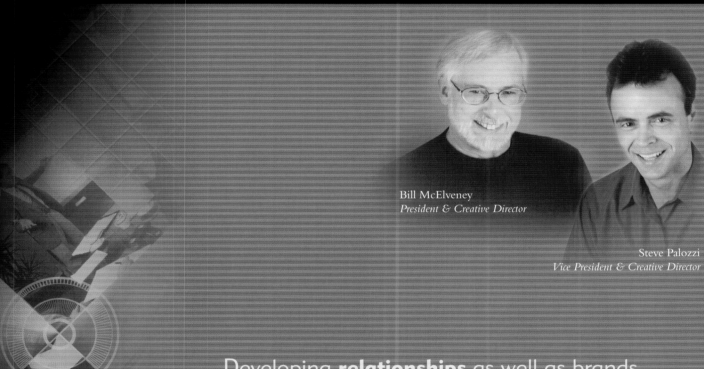

Bill McElveney
President & Creative Director

Steve Palozzi
Vice President & Creative Director

Developing **relationships** as well as brands

Adopting your **challenges** and making them our own

Establishing that **creativity** has value

CORPORATE & CONSUMER PRODUCT BRANDING • ADVERTISING DESIGN • PACKAGE DESIGN • WEB DESIGN

Riveredge Resort
Corporate Identity
Advertising Design
Website Design
Photography

NEW YORK'S Finger Lakes

Destination Branding

New York's Finger Lakes
Corporate Identity
Collateral Materials
Advertising Design
Merchandise

Corporate Branding

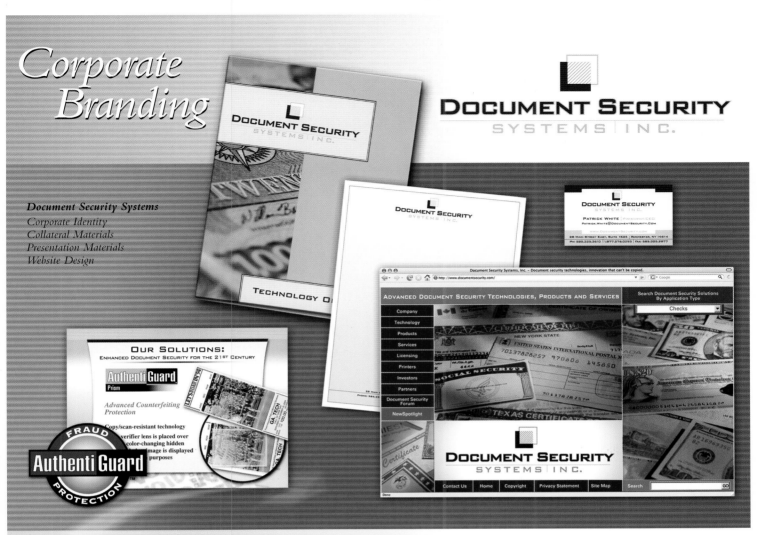

Document Security Systems
Corporate Identity
Collateral Materials
Presentation Materials
Website Design

Badger Technologies
Corporate Identity
Collateral Materials
Website Design
Photography

3

FLAVOR ADVISORY INTENSE CONTENT

DRINK IT UP!

Available in Ori... Flavor and NEW L...

InTense MILKS

Upstate Farms Intense Milk
Product Branding
Label Design
Marketing Materials

CAUTION: DOUBLE DIP ZONE

(PLEASE DIP RESPONSIBLY)

BISON French Onion DIP

BISON Nacho Jalapeño DIP

BISON Salsa Dip

BISON Creamy Ranch DIP

UPSTATE FARMS · GENERATIONS OF QUALITY ®

Upstate Farms Bison Sour Cream Dip
Fleet Graphics
Billboards

It's not the chip. It's the Dip!

BISON WITH FRESH SOUR CREAM French Onion...

Upstate Farms Promotional Items

A. Promotional Graphics
B. Non-fat Yogurt Brochure
C. Yogurt Poster
D. 4 oz. Yogurt Carton Design
E. Fleet Graphics

A

B

C

D

E

5

A

B

Consumer Product Branding

C

A. **Sun Orchard Brand**
   Harvest Cuts Premium Sliced Apples

B. **Wagner Valley Brewing Co.**
   India Pale Ale

C. **Great Lakes Kraut**
   Krrrrisp Kraut Sauerkraut

D. **Uncle Wally's**
   Smart Portion Muffins
   Oven Luv'n Muffins

D

1

2

3

4

5

6

7

8

9

10

Corporate Identity

1. **Atwater Foods, Inc.**
   Premium Dried Fruit Producer

2. **Wisner & Wisner, LLP**
   DWI Attorneys

3. **Big Kids Club**
   Agency Promotional Logo

4. **The Lodge at Woodcliff**
   Resort and Conference Center

5. **Xelus**
   Service Optimization Corporation

6. **Gravure**
   Gravure Magazine Masthead

7. **LeRoy Village Green**
   Residential Healthcare Facility

8. **Warm Lake Estate**
   Winery and Vineyards

9. **Michael Shea's Irish Amber**
   High Falls Brewing Company

10. **Wagner Valley India Pale Ale**
    Wagner Valley Brewing Company

McElveney & Palozzi Design Group, Inc. 255

Website Design

A. Bausch & Lomb

B. NECA/IBEW Electrical Contractors

C. Richards & West Manufacturing

D. Maritime Intelligence

McElveney & Palozzi
DESIGN GROUP INC.

1255 University Avenue | Suite 200 | Rochester, NY 14607 | Phone: 585-473-7630 | www.mandpdesign.com

950 Sixth Avenue : Ste. 212
San Diego, CA 92101
619 234 1211
free 877 234 1211
www.thinkmorris.com

Design without strategy is a
commodity. Our strength is
serving your brand through
the thinking that takes place
behind the design. Our
focus is on the consumer
experience.

From product launches
to brand revitalization to
integrated campaigns,
Morris! Communication
creates strategic cross-media
branding for youth-minded
and enjoyment brands.

: brand strategy
: identity
: web
: motion & video
: collateral
: advertising

the
power of
design
can...

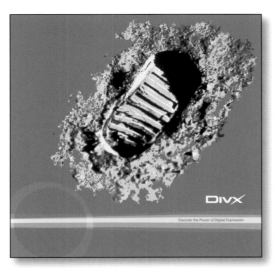

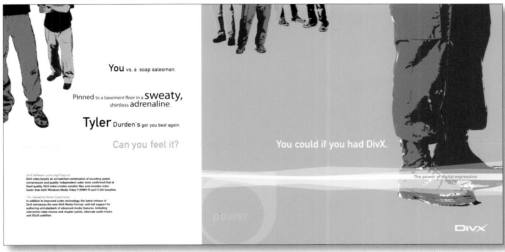

You vs. a soap salesman.

Pinned to a basement floor in a **sweaty,** shirtless **adrenaline.**

Tyler Durden's got you beat again.

Can you feel it?

You could if you had DivX.

The power of digital expression

DivX Software Licensing Program
DivX video boasts an unmatched combination of encoding speed, compression and quality. Independent codec tests confirmed that at fixed quality, DivX video creates smaller files and encodes video faster than both Windows Media Video 9 (WMV-9) and H.264 baseline.

The Interactive Media Experience
In addition to improved codec technology, the latest release of DivX introduces the new DivX Media Format, with full support for authoring and playback of advanced media features, including interactive video menus and chapter points, alternate audio tracks and XSUB subtitles.

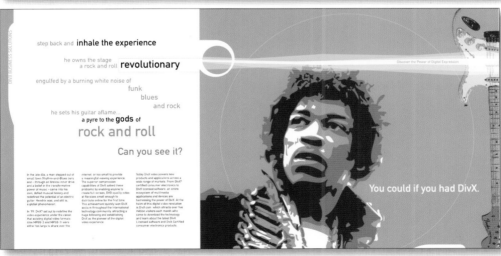

step back and **inhale the experience**

he owns the stage
a rock and roll **revolutionary**

engulfed by a burning white noise of
funk
blues
and rock

he sets his guitar aflame...
a pyre to the gods of
rock and roll

Can you see it?

Discover the Power of Digital Expression

You could if you had DivX.

In the late 60s, a man stepped out of small town Rhythm-and-Blues bars and – through an intense inner drive and a belief in the transformative power of music – came into his own, defied musical history and redefined the potential of an electric guitar. Hendrix was, and still is, a global phenomenon.

In '99, DivX set out to redefine the video experience under the canon that existing digital video formats (like MPEG-2 and MPEG-1) were either too large to share over the internet, or too small to provide a meaningful viewing experience. The superior compression capabilities of DivX solved these problems by enabling anyone to create full-screen, DVD-quality video at file sizes small enough to distribute online for the first time. This achievement quickly won DivX accls.in throughout the international technology community, attracting a huge following and establishing DivX as the pioneer of the digital video experience.

Today DivX video powers new products and applications across a wide range of markets. From DivX® certified consumer electronics to DivX Licensed software, an entire ecosystem of multimedia applications and devices are harnessing the power of DivX. At the helm of this digital video revolution is DivX.com, which attracts over five million visitors each month who come to download the latest DivX Licensed software and DivX Certified consumer electronics products.

deliver digital expression.

DivX

strategic brand revitalization :
branding, collateral, environment & web

the power of design can
launch a new era.

San Diego Chargers

brand (identity & uniform)
revitalization launch :
branding, web & advertising

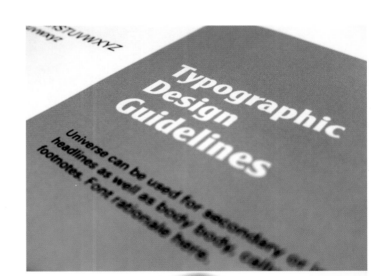

Typographic Design Guidelines

Universe can be used for secondary or body headlines as well as body body, (all-time footnotes. Font rationale here.

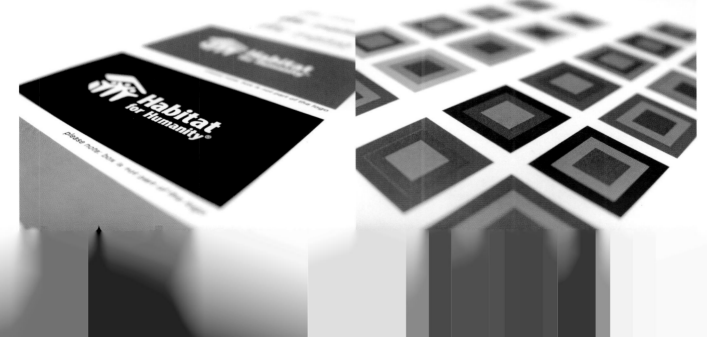

please note, this is not part of the logo

make a passion portable.

Upper Deck Entertainment

World of Warcraft
Trading Card Game :
branding, print, POP, advertising & web

Morris! Communication

Gingerbread Man movie :
branding, video, motion graphics & web

the power of design can

create a cultural icon.

Optima Soulsight is a group of global reach agency partners in North America, Latin America, Europe, Asia and Africa. We offer a full range of integrated brand consulting and creative design services. Our focus is on identifying each brands' greatest potential and elevating the brand experience through smart, intuitive creative solutions.

optimasoulsight.com   847.681.4444

Coca-Cola Holiday International

Lipton Select Premium Infusion Teas

Lake Champlain Premium Chocolates

Back to Nature

Miller Lite, Miller Genuine Draft, Miller Chill, and Icehouse

Peterson Ray & Company
311 N. Market Street, Suite 311
Dallas, TX 75202
214.954.0522
www.peterson.com

Peterson Ray & Company takes pride in its award-winning record, spanning over two decades, of partnering with corporations and universities to create successful marketing communications. We have invested heavily in developing our expertise, nurturing our talents, and keeping pace with technology to better serve our clients. We conscientiously strive to understand your history and culture in order to produce communications that effectively target your audience.

As a result, clients large and small rely on us for a broad range of materials, including recruitment materials, annual reports, corporate identities, websites, marketing and capabilities brochures, sales collateral, advertising, alumni magazines, and research. Whatever the project, our success means creating thoughtful, innovative communications that exceed your expectations.

"All in Good Time."

Cervantes

You

matter.

Take a good look at George Fox University. See if we fit your goals and ambitions.

You and your future matter to us.

Meet your future.

SINCE 1891, George Fox has prepared its graduates to be people of influence throughout the world. Choose from more than 30 majors and 45 minors to fulfill your career goals. Our programs range from social science to natural science, mathematics and computers, to business and economics. Several paths provide leadership opportunities. *U.S. News & World Report* has repeatedly ranked George Fox as a top-tier regional university, and as a "best value" in its category.

The twelve most-often-asked questions about tuition and financial aid.

be all

Wait. There's more. We can't possibly give you the whole picture or answer all your questions in a brochure. Check our Web site and call one of our counselors for a personal overview of George Fox. Then visit our campus, talk with faculty and students, sit in on classes and stay overnight. All it takes is a phone call or e-mail. We'll show you in person what students love about George Fox University.

Be here.

GEORGE FOX
UNIVERSITY

GEORGE FOX
UNIVERSITY

Office of Undergraduate Admissions
414 N. Meridian Street
Newberg, Oregon 97132

be
here.

A PARENT

What
parent n
know ab
university

George F

What every parent
should know about G

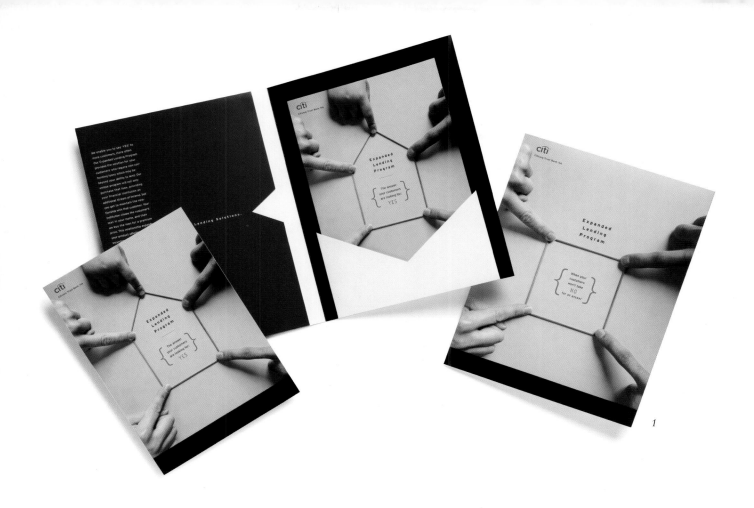

1 Citibank, lending program pocket folder and brochure
2 Baylor College of Dentistry, centennial history book
3 Music Road Records
4 Love from A to Z
5 George Fox University Athletics

1

FOSTERING LEADERSHIP AT ALL LEVELS

2

REEL TEXAS AND A "GIANT" MYTH

3

A LOVE Story

NOVELIST REFLECTS
ON A WANDERING EYE,
GETTERS AT SOFTBALL,
AND A MEN FOR FOR LIFE

4

fashion art

1

1 Centex annual report
2 Dallas Society of Visual Communications, Rough magazine

2

1 Bob Childers, Restless Spirit CD
2 HomeTeam Pest Defense logo
3 Crossroads Coffeehouse and Music logo
4 Brinker International Annual Reports

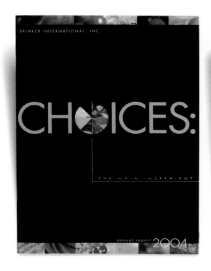

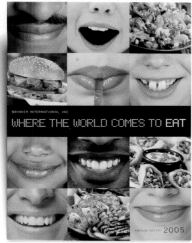

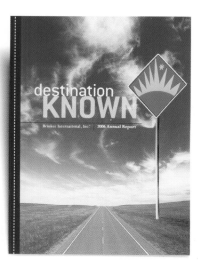

4

Seton Hall University, recruitment materials

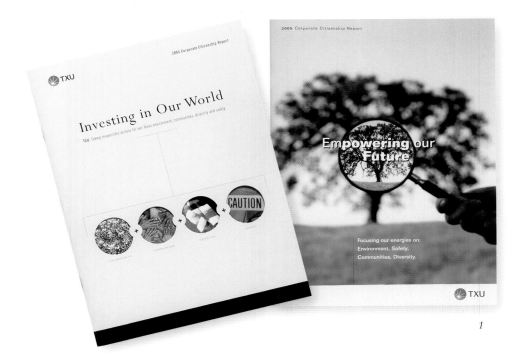

1 TXU, Corporate Citizenship Reports
2 Jimmy LaFave, Cactus Cafe poster
3 Dallas Society of Visual Communications, Crawfish Madness poster

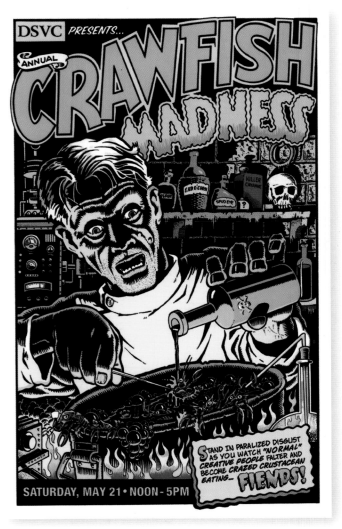

DICK & JANE//See Dick shop. See Jane accessorize. Dick & Jane is a merchant of classic, metropolitan style for men and women. The objective: establish the visual language for Dick & Jane through a multi-purpose identity system. Planet solution: address the classic boy/girl narrative through pairings of found images of male and female iconography. The nostalgic imagery turns business cards, hangtags, packaging, signage, and ads into a playful dialogue between the masculine and the feminine.

CANDINAS//Swiss-trained chocolatier Markus Candinas loved the tasteful, foil-free packaging Planet designed for him a dozen years ago when he set up shop. But when he recently updated the shape of his chocolates from squares and spheres and rectangles to the single, opulent "squircle," he asked us to refresh his packaging as well. The updated system of elegant, understated packaging conveys the rich and refined nature of the chocolates it contains.

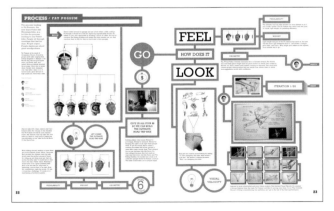

GARY FISHER MOUNTAIN BIKES//In mountain biking circles, Gary Fisher is The Man. Circa '77, along with a few shaggy friends atop even shaggier northern California terrain, Gary dreamed up a pastime that became a sport that has become a lifestyle for millions. Along the way, the man also became a brand, and today Gary Fisher is firmly entrenched as "The First and Last Name in Mountain Biking." Since 2001, Planet has been charged with building upon the legend, keeping watch over Fisher's unique personality and stewarding its alternative position in the market. From the alternatively-formatted Gary Fisher catalog (an iconic piece in the industry) to the website, advertising, product launch films, in-store materials, and a revolutionary multi-media dealer training tool, Planet has shaped the brand in Gary's image on all fronts.

PUNCHSTOCK AND UPPERCUT IMAGES//Sister brands PunchStock (royalty-free stock imagery) and UpperCut (rights-managed stock photography) stand out among their rivals in the fiercely competitive field of stock imagery. Planet has helped craft both style-conscious brands from the ground up, from their pugilistic names to their made-you-look promo vehicles and online presence. Our latest offering: the punch-out magnet sheets shown at top, which drove recipients to a promotional minisite of animated shorts.

MEASURE FOR MEASURE

by WILLIAM SHAKESPEARE
directed by KENNETH ALBERS

• • • • • • • • • •

In this outrageous comedy, the arrogance of power runs amok among the affairs of church and state. Neither of which escape Shakespeare's engaging, scathing satire brought to you by a fascinating group of characters unlike any other in the world of Bard-dom.

Vienna's become a Sin City of moral decay and decadence. The ruling Duke's lost control, leaves town suddenly, leaving his Deputy in charge to clean up the mess. At least that's what everyone thinks. The Duke actually stays around in a monk's disguise, spends the play pulling strings in the wings.

Meanwhile, the Deputy unleashes the vice squad on iniquity's dens. Problem is he can't seem to control his own secret passion. When a nun named Isabella shows up to plead for her condemned brother's life, he agrees to a pardon provided she agrees to sleep with him. That's when the fireworks begin. Before they end, we've got a severely severed head, a switcheroo in bed and enough power abuse to cook that Deputy's goose.

What bark. What bite. This play's got fantastical powers to incite. With Jim DeVita as the Deputy taking a run at Colleen Madden the nun, while Brian Robert Mani looks on as the Duke in disguise. Sarah Day plays the Madame of Tarts with a tongue that's sharp and Paul Bentzen's a revered advisor worth listening to. Grabbing great seats now is definitely the thing to do. ❋ OPENS JUNE 29

ROMEO AND JULIET

by WILLIAM SHAKESPEARE
directed by DAVID FRANK

• • • • • • • • • •

If ever there's a place to see the world's greatest love story it's here at a theatre in the woods. Where the heavens are star-cross'd o'er head and the moon beams at the mere mention of Romeo and Juliet.

Theirs is a love we long for in our dreams. So pure and uncompromisingly deep. Rises above life's pitfalls, all pettiness and dangers, even death itself.

Juliet is the youngest and most innocent of Shakespeare's heroines. Through her union with Romeo, this play becomes a glorious, lyrical hymn to everything youthful and idealistic. A work in which the Bard's genius reaches first full flowering in language and storytelling power. Brought alive with the clarity, simplicity in which we take such pride.

Surrounding these immortal lovers are vivid, worldly characters drawn from the prime of our acting company. Tracy Michelle Arnold is Juliet's lifelong nurse, David Daniel the hot-tempered Tybalt and Jonathan Smoots that fatal friar. Mother Nature plays an all-embracing role. With piercing starlight. Warm, perfumed breezes. Mysterious, erotic nights. An amazing setting in which to experience this show.

A story so passionately told, swelling so bold in pageantry, gorgeous costuming, cold steel hotly clashing. With action thundering up and down the aisles and love's tender bloom aglow in yon window. ❋ OPENS JUNE 24

ARMS AND THE MAN

by GEORGE BERNARD SHAW
directed by JAMES BOHNEN

• • • • • • • • • •

A young woman alone in a dark bedroom. Gunfire explodes in the streets below. She cringes in fear as the shutters slowly pull open and the figure of a man clambers inside.

Thus begins one delightful comedy on the absurdities of love and war. Opened to raves in London, 1894. Hugely popular to this day. Welcome aboard. You're in for quite a treat as our acting company sinks its talents into a world famous show.

Colleen Madden plays Raina, the woman above whose romantic notion of love (and war) is stood on its head when Jim DeVita, a desperate, beaten soldier on the run, climbs in through that bedroom window. What fun. Tricky part is, her fiancée fights for the other side. A ridiculously courageous cavalryman. Preening peacock besides.

You'll have an ache in your side bursting with mirth as this threesome entangles itself in Raina's lovably dysfunctional family. Sarah Day is her snob of a mom. Paul Bentzen's the dad, a Major who's majorly befuddled. Their maid is one volatile volcanic eruption.

Shaw's a play writing genius for sure. His work lyric with wisdom, hilarity and charm. The repartee sings. Laughing, your spirit will wing. Leaving you feeling so light on your feet you just might glide down the hill to the parking lot after. ❋ OPENS AUGUST 12

JULIUS CAESAR

by WILLIAM SHAKESPEARE
directed by SANFORD ROBBINS

• • • • • • • • • •

Thrill to the action up the hill. Feel its fervid pulse beat. The pounding of destiny beneath your feet. This gripping political thriller spins such a web of intrigue, you're quickly and totally immersed in a mesmerizing spectacle.

Find yourself among cheering, enthusiastic crowds welcoming Mighty Caesar home to Rome in triumph.

Bug-shrieking night reaches hysterical pitch as the conspirators converge around Brutus and Cassius, tightening the knot of their deadly plot. You are caught in shock and awe as the assassins converge, slashing open the Emperor.

Spellbinding. Mark Antony pours his heart out over Caesar's dead body. Inciting the mob into murderous riot, hell bent on revenge. Sweeps you along to barren battlefields where those murderers meet an ignominious end.

Their noble ideals could never justify the means of that single act of savagery. Indeed, from ancient Rome to now, this is a work for our time, for all time. In a world whose history continues to be written in blood.

The rock solid core of our acting company has been cast. With Brian Robert Mani as Caesar, David Daniel as Mark Antony, Jonathan Smoots as Brutus and Tracy Michelle Arnold as his wife Portia.

From the beautiful soaring of its language to the profound psychological ache embedded in its soul, this is one powerful show. ❋ OPENS AUGUST 19

APT//Planet has designed the American Players Theatre season promotional materials for the past 17 years, and it's always one of our favorite projects. The 2006 Book of Summer (preseason brochure) is a celebration of the play-in-the-woods appeal of the APT experience: driving through rolling rural hills, dining alfresco on wine and cheese, walking uphill at sunset through lush summer woods to the intimate outdoor amphitheater, and watching classical theater late into the night. Planet conjured up a world, rendered in woodcut, in which a tree serves as a metaphor for stage and theater, while birds take seat in the audience or play a more active role in the season's theatrical tales.

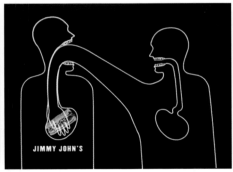

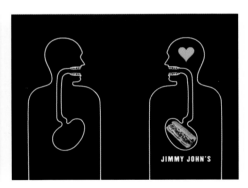

JIMMY JOHN'S GOURMET SANDWICHES//Jimmy John's is unlike any sub shop in the industry: no games, no gimmicks, just good, old-fashioned, homemade sandwiches made from fresh-baked bread, all-natural meats, and vegetables sliced fresh daily at each restaurant. Founded in 1983 by 19-year-old Jimmy John Liautaud in a converted garage in Charleston, Illinois, Jimmy John's has grown to more than 480 corporate and franchised locations in more than 34 states and two countries. Planet Propaganda has been an integral part of this growth since 1999, creating a constant barrage of messages in stores and through extensive print, radio, television, and outdoor advertising. Planet has firmly established a brand image and personality that mimics the founder's maniacal obsession for quality, flawless execution and a bigger-than-life approach to business and pleasure.

BRETFORD FURNITURE//Bretford, a 60-year-old family-run contract furniture manufacturer, turned to Planet Propaganda for a new brand image that would appeal to the aesthetically charged architecture and interior design community. Planet conducted a thorough analysis of Bretford's product, clients, and corporate culture, and distilled the brand ethos down to a new tag, A Higher Form of Function, and a clean, elegant visual vocabulary. The new brand image was reflected in a logo and award-winning website (bretford.com), as well as sales tools, national advertising, and showroom design. Bretford's new image caused quite a buzz in the business. It even caught the eye of industry style arbiter Herman Miller, who has since formed a strategic marketing alliance with Bretford based in no small part on the strength of Bretford's marketing identity.

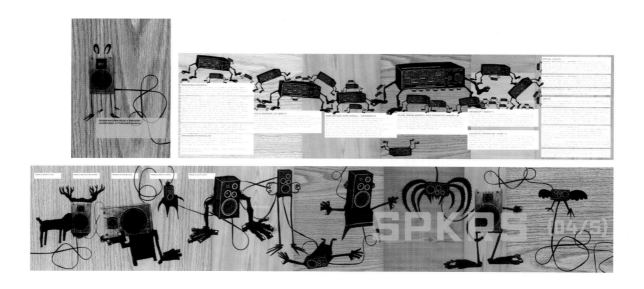

DESIGN MADISON//This professional association of designers, art directors, and assorted other creatives relies on its seasonal marketing materials to help draw members of the local design community to upcoming events. Planet took the literal approach to generate interest in the season's speaker lineup. Hand-drawn stereophonic speaker monsters cavort in wood-paneled comfort on the speaker brochure and grace actual plywood slabs on the screen-printed season posters.

Pressley Jacobs: a design partnership

230 West Superior, 7th Floor
Chicago, IL 60610
312.640.0679
www.pressleyjacobs.com

In business, success requires effective communications.

Effective communications depend upon developing strong relationships.

The strongest relationship in business is a partnership.

Pressley Jacobs is a design *partnership*. What sets us apart is our commitment to working with our clients, colleagues and project teams. To bring brands and businesses to life.

Partnerships begin with understanding. We take the time to learn our clients' organizations and audiences — their objectives, cultures, and concerns. The knowledge we gain translates into sound strategies and compelling ideas. Communications are clear and consistent. Every word and image connects — and counts.

Successful partnerships last. Since 1985, we have built long-term relationships with a diverse group of clients, from start-ups and not-for-profits to FORTUNE 100 companies. And their referrals are the primary source of new business relationships. There's no better measure of the value of our partnerships. Or our success.

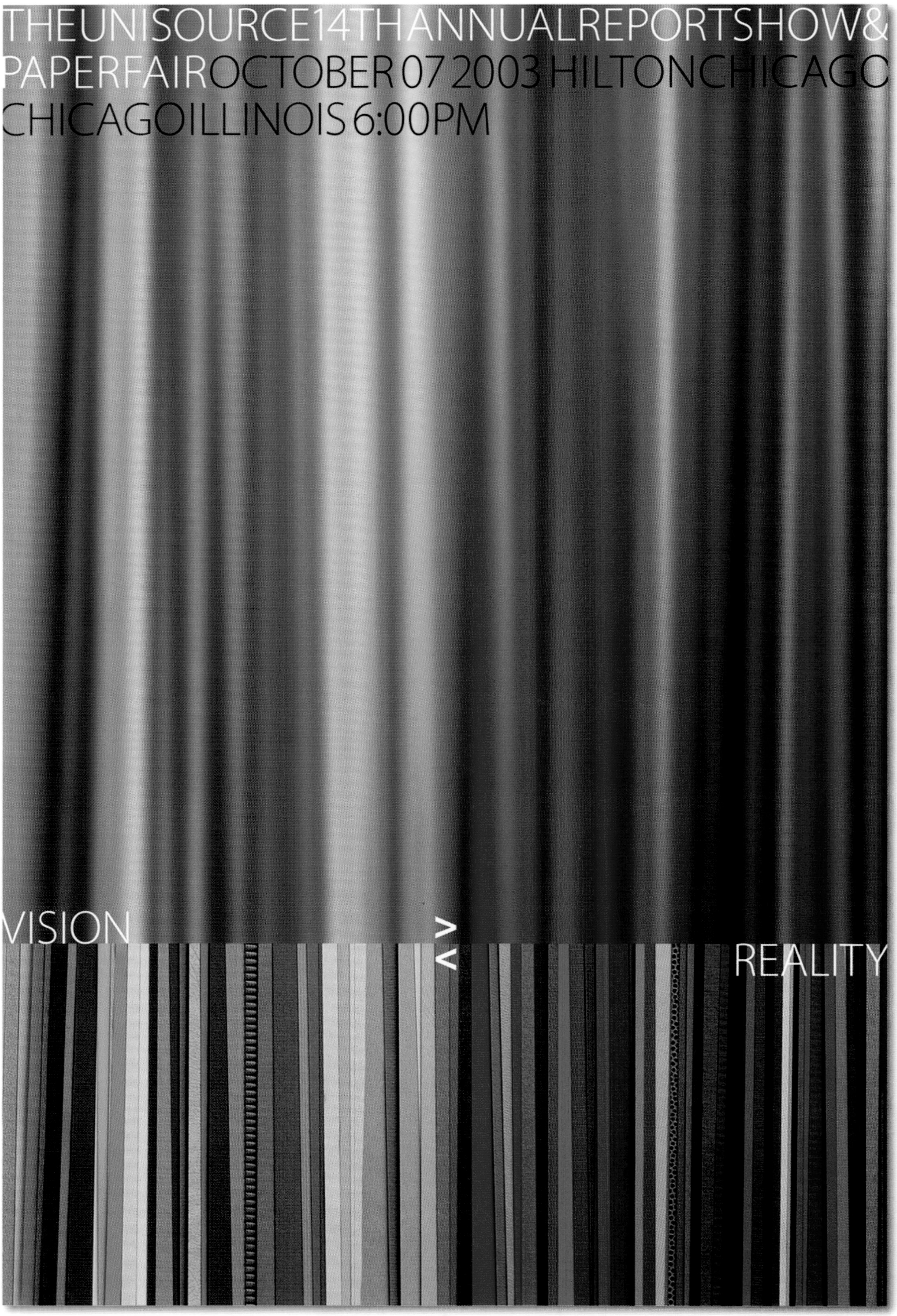

THEUNISOURCE14THANNUALREPORTSHOW&
PAPERFAIROCTOBER 07 2003 HILTONCHICAGO
CHICAGOILLINOIS 6:00PM

VISION

>
> >

REALITY

resource

synXis

HR@M.

IMA

(left page)
Unisource, paper merchant
Event poster

InSite
THE EMPLOYEE INTRANET

Employee Name

Getting Started   Latest Headlines

LIGHT TAN

DARK BLUE
Print:
Pentone 2685 C
C 100

BROWN
Print:
Pentone 462 C
C 50

DARK BROWN
Print:
Pentone 7533 C
Pentone 7533 U

Accent Colors

DARK TEAL **TEAL**
Pentone 5463 C Pentone 5473 C

DARK GREEN **GREEN**
Pentone 5743 C

TAN **LIGHT TAN**
Pentone 466 C Pentone 468 C

DARK RUST **RED**
Pentone 1817 C

DARK RUST **RUST**
Pentone 174 C Pentone 471 C

LIGHT GRAY

Hudson

地域検索： Japan - Japanese

検索条件： キーワードを入力してくだ

ハドソンについて

ハドソンのサー

正社員の採用

人材採用プロセス？

シング

ハドソンのトレント

CRITICAL
THINKING

HUDSON THOUGHT LEADERSHIP SERIES

2
1

p.4
**Sarbanes-Oxley
Year One:**
COMPANIES FIND SOME GOOD
WITH THE BAD AND THE UGLY

p.16
**The Internet
Comes of Age**
FOR THE RECRUITMENT INDUSTRY

p.20
Offshoring
FOR COMPETITIVE ADVANTAGE

Program includes marketing communications, advertising, Websites, employee communications, annual reports, event materials, thoughtpapers, exhibit displays, electronic and video presentations, online brand guidelines and image bank.

(top left clockwise)

1 *Sparkplug, business broadband internet provider*
   Interactive marketing

2 *Resource Graphic, print management company*
   Website

3 *Winnetka Public School Nursery, preschool*
   Website

4 *Equity Office Properties Trust, commercial real estate company*
   Interactive marketing

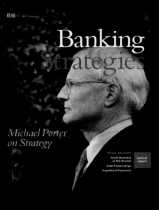

BAI

Banking
Strategies

*Michael Porter
on Strategy*

RETAIL BUSINESS
**Small Business
at the Branch**
ATM Partnerships
Expedited Payments

special
report

BAI

Banking
Strategies

special
report

RETAIL DELIVERY
PART II
The Frontline Experience
GIVE THE CUSTOMERS WHAT THEY WANT

in this issue:
**Customers and
Their Checks**
Authentication
Data Auditing

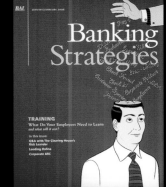

BAI

Banking
Strategies

TRAINING
*What Do Your Employees Need to Learn
and what will it cost?*

in this issue:
**Q&A with The Clearing House's
Rick Leander**
Lending Online
Corporate ARC

BAI

Banking
Strategies

SURVIVING
IN THE
MIDDLE
Aubrey Patterson's BancorpSouth

in this issue:
Small Business Deposits
The Top Minimums
of Returns
Tax Capture

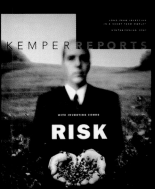

KEMPER**REPORTS**

LONG-TERM INVESTING
IN A SHORT-TERM WORLD?
WINTER/SPRING 2001

WITH INVESTING COMES
RISK

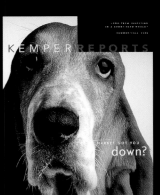

KEMPER**REPORTS**

LONG-TERM INVESTING
IN A SHORT-TERM WORLD?
SUMMER/FALL 2000

MARKET GOT YOU
down?

KEMPER**REPORTS**

LONG-TERM INVESTING
IN A SHORT-TERM WORLD?
SPECIAL EDITION 2000

College?
An early start will help her reach her goal

KEMPER**REPORTS**

LONG-TERM INVESTING
IN A SHORT-TERM WORLD?
FALL/WINTER 1997

got the
TAXPAYER
Blues?

Capital
GAINS
One Hit Wapit, Two Hit Low
and three, Nine Band

Luminary holiday greeting, following September 11
Self promotion

Partial Client List:

	Hallmark	*Learning Point Associates*	*The ROC Group*	*Standfast Packaging*
	Hanley-Wood, Inc.	*Leo Burnett*	*Ryerson, Inc.*	*Tellabs*
Advocate Health Care	*Heidrick & Struggles*	*MaxJazz*	*S.C. Johnson & Son, Inc.*	*Tribune Company*
American Library Assoc.	*Hewitt Associates*	*McDonald's Corporation*	*Sabre Holdings Corporation*	*UBS*
BAI	*Hudson*	*Motorola*	*Scudder Investments*	*Unisource*
Chicago Board of Trade	*Indianapolis Museum of Art*	*Northern Trust Company*	*The Segal Company*	*U.S. Army Reserve*
Corus Bankshares	*Kemper Funds*	*Northwestern Memorial Hosp.*	*Sibson Consulting*	*University of Chicago*
Equity Group Investments	*Kraft General Foods*	*Platinum Technology, Inc.*	*Snap-On Incorporated*	*Watson Wyatt Worldwide*
Equity Office Properties Trust	*Kraft Foodservice*	*Primedia*	*SPSS Inc.*	*William Blair & Company*
Grubb & Ellis	*The Lakota Group*	*Resource Graphic*	*SparkPlug*	*William Mercer, Inc.*

range
105 turtle creek blvd.
dallas, texas 75207
214.744.0555

range nw
409 coeur d'alene ave.
coeur d'alene, idaho 83814
208.667.0201

rangeus.com

range is all about reach. it's about the restlessness of the human spirit to find a new idea. a fresh approach. a better way. as innovative thinkers we view the ability to align your business strategy with the power of creative vision as the most important factor in achieving success. it's not something we take on faith. it's something we've learned from experience.

identity. marketing. interactive. product. environment. motion.

THE BOSTON PHILHARMONIC 2006 ART OF POSSIBILITY GALA
WITH BENJAMIN ZANDER
SATURDAY, APRIL 1, 2006
5:30PM DOORS OPEN
MEMORIAL HALL AT HARVARD UNIVERSITY
6PM ART OF POSSIBILITY PRESENTATION, SANDERS THEATRE
8PM COCKTAILS AND DINNER, ANNENBERG HALL
9PM DANCING AND LIVE AUCTION

THE ART OF
Possibility

Ross is a brand-building agency
where outstanding creative begins
with strong research and strategy.
In other words, our job starts with
understanding our clients.

We found the place where branding begins.

The better we understand the
companies we work for, the
more accurately we can anticipate
the needs of their audiences.
And the more efficiently we can
craft communications and
tactics to reach the right people.

By starting with understanding,
we make sure our job ends with results.

R⊕SS

OBEY
YOUR
BRAND

MANAGE
YOUR
BRAND

REWARD
YOUR
BRAND

Ross
305 SW Water St.
4th Floor
Peoria, IL 61602
309.680.4131
www.rosscps.com

228 BEERS CAN BE OVERWHELMING

PEORIA JAYCEES PRESENT

2006 INTERNATIONAL
BEER FESTIVAL

APRIL 21-ST. JUDE'S NIGHT 6 TO 10 PM   APRIL 22-MAIN EVENT 1 TO 9 PM

EXPO GARDENS

PEORIABEERFEST.COM

DRINK BEER FOR GOOD, NOT EVIL
FRIDAY, APRIL 21, ST. JUDE'S CHARITY NIGHT. FOR MORE INFORMATION GO TO PEORIABEERFEST.COM

PEORIA JAYCEES PRESENT
2006 INTERNATIONAL
BEER FESTIVAL
APRIL 21-ST. JUDE'S NIGHT 6 TO 10 PM   APRIL 22-MAIN EVENT 1 TO 9 PM
EXPO GARDENS
PEORIABEERFEST.COM

IN EUROPE, BEER BELLIES ARE SEXY
PEORIABEERFEST.COM

PEORIA JAYCEES PRESENT
2006 INTERNATIONAL
BEER FESTIVAL
APRIL 21-ST. JUDE'S NIGHT 6 TO 10 PM   APRIL 22-MAIN EVENT 1 TO 9 PM
EXPO GARDENS

THINK YOUR GIRLFRIEND'S TOO FAT?
NOW'S A GOOD TIME TO TELL HER.
PEORIABEERFEST.COM

PEORIA JAYCEES PRESENT
2006 INTERNATIONAL
BEER FESTIVAL
APRIL 21-ST. JUDE'S NIGHT 6 TO 10 PM   APRIL 22-MAIN EVENT 1 TO 9 PM
EXPO GARDENS

The Peoria International Beer Fest is one of the largest beer festivals in the nation. Ross created a complete campaign including T-shirts, posters, POP and radio.

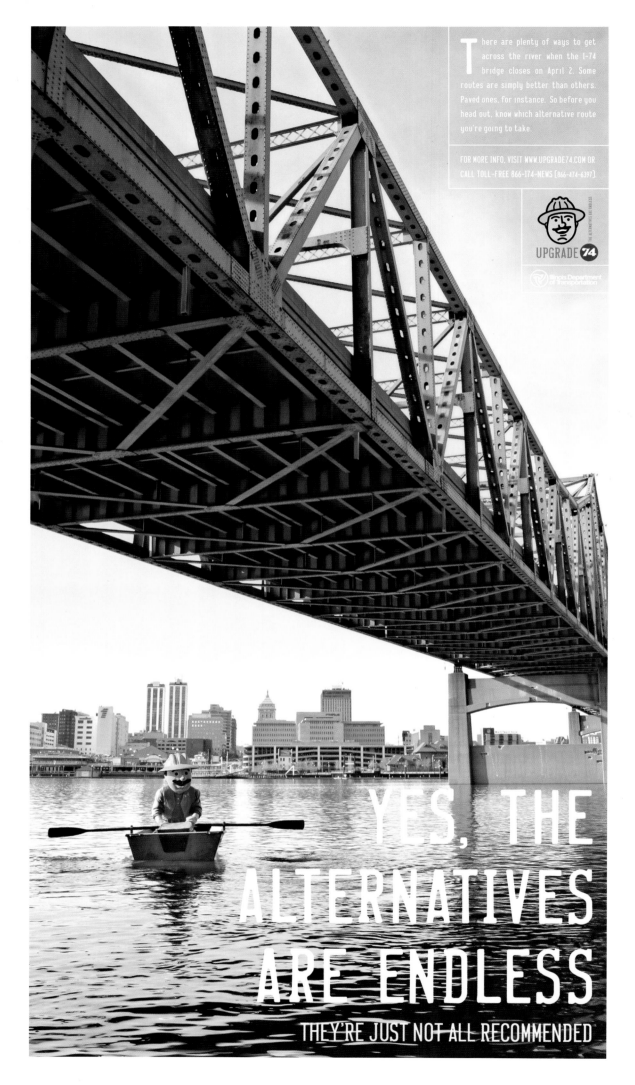

For our public awareness campaign addressing a massive overhaul of Peoria's interstate system, Ross worked in traditional and nontraditional media, creating road signs, print ads, fridge magnets, air fresheners and live appearances, all branded with IDOT's "Jack Hammer" mascot.

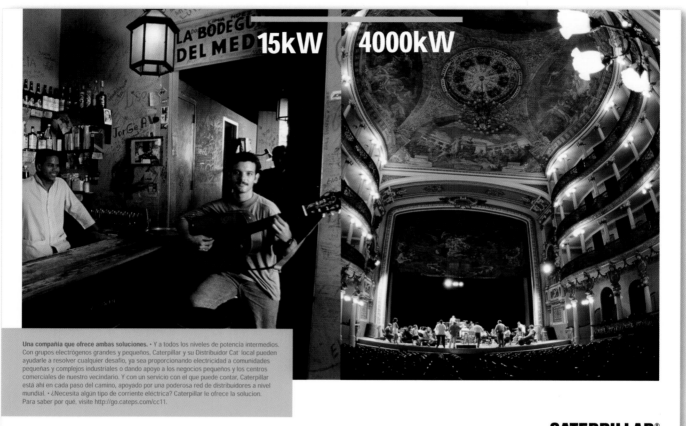

Una compañía que ofrece ambas soluciones. • Y a todos los niveles de potencia intermedios. Con grupos electrógenos grandes y pequeños, Caterpillar y su Distribuidor Cat local pueden ayudarle a resolver cualquier desafío, ya sea proporcionando electricidad a comunidades pequeñas y complejos industriales o dando apoyo a los negocios pequeños y los centros comerciales de nuestro vecindario. Y con un servicio con el que puede contar, Caterpillar está ahí en cada paso del camino, apoyado por una poderosa red de distribuidores a nivel mundial. • ¿Necesita algún tipo de corriente eléctrica? Caterpillar le ofrece la solución. Para saber por qué, visite http://go.cateps.com/cc11.

CATERPILLAR®
TODAY'S WORK. TOMORROW'S WORLD.™

Our global ad campaign for Caterpillar® Electric Power emphasized the scope of the company's generator offerings and was versatile enough to be relevant on six continents.

For the worldwide launch of the Caterpillar C175 generator set, Ross created multiple materials, including the invitations and an outdoor light display branding the event.

THERE'S MORE TO GOODWILL THAN YOU THINK.

2nd Annual Goodwill Gala
May 5, 2006
Peoria Civic Center - $100 per plate
Proceeds go toward the operation and
maintenance of Goodwill's Home for Veterans.
For more information call (309) 682-1113

Schwartz Brand Group
611 Broadway, Suite 430
New York, NY 10012
212-925-6460
SchwartzBrandGroup.com

S|B|G

Schwartz Brand Group is an award-winning branding and creative services consultancy. We help businesses grow by partnering with clients to develop and implement integrated communications systems. Our work unites the disciplines of brand development, corporate identity, print & interactive design, communications strategy and advertising.

SIMULATION REPORT AND SUMMARY OF FIND...

of nine former White House cabinet and senior national security officials c...
a simulated working group of a White House cabinet. Their task: to advi...
as the nation grapples with an oil crisis over a seven-month period. As th...
unaware of the circumstances or nature of the oil crisis.

...CURING AMERICA'S
...TURE ENERGY FOUNDATION

2555 PENNSYLVANIA AVE NW
SUITE 719
WASHINGTON, DC 20037

Securing America's
Future Energy

Wha
$120
for th
cond

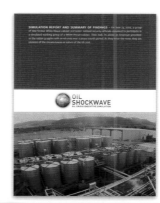

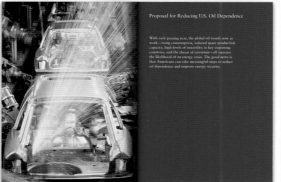

Helping Solve America's Energy Crisis | Securing America's Future Energy is a leading voice on the economic and national security implications of U.S. oil dependence, promoting sustainable alternatives. SBG develops integrated brand strategy across all communications touchpoints, uniting SAFE's message and creating action—regionally, nationally, and globally.

Creating Connections | Agency Access provides integrated marketing services for commercial artists, connecting them with ad agencies, design firms, and other buyers worldwide. SBG partners with the company to develop brand strategy, identity design, and cross-media communications that align both the brand and business with the creatives they serve.

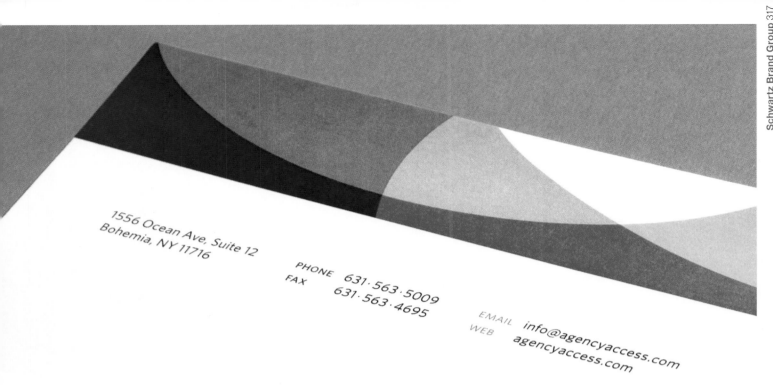

1556 Ocean Ave, Suite 12
Bohemia, NY 11716

PHONE   631·563·5009
FAX   631·563·4695

EMAIL   info@agencyaccess.com
WEB   agencyaccess.com

agencyaccess

1556 Ocean Ave, Suite 12
Bohemia, NY 11716

PHONE   631·563·5009
FAX   631·563·4695

EMAIL   inf
WEB   age

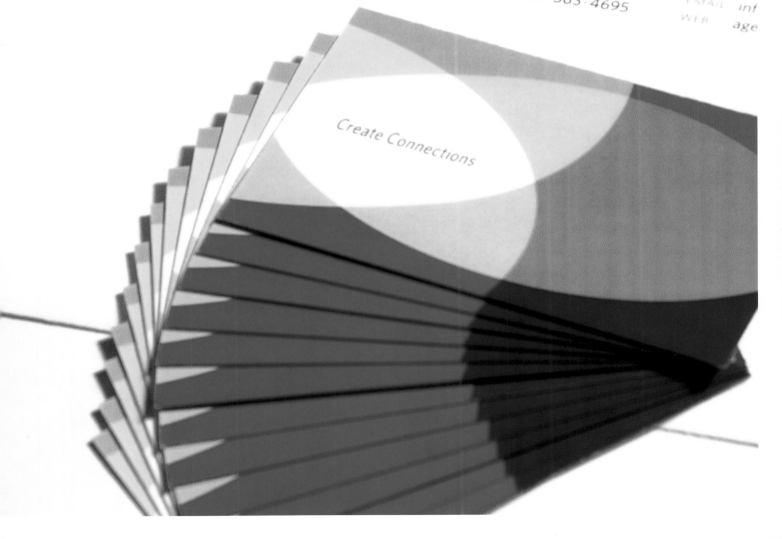

Create Connections

We Develop Integrated Brands...

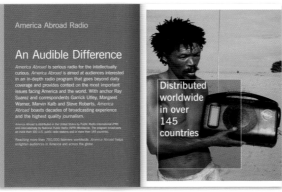
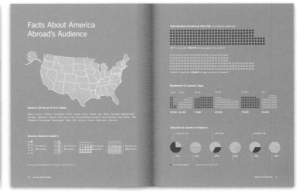

...in Print The permanence of print is unique in its ability to create a lasting impression. We help clients make the most out of their print communications, by uniting medium and message through compelling content, distinctive design, and a meticulous focus on craftsmanship. Every physical detail reinforces the brand to create strong, emotional connections.

...and Online Developing an effective interactive strategy is about more than design and technology. It's about creating valuable online experiences that align business and user goals. We help clients execute online by applying deep expertise in information architecture, usability design, and interactive development to create valuable user experiences.

"I've worked in financial services marketing for 10+ years. During that time, SBG has been one of the few agencies who truly listen, then develop and deliver an executable solution the first time out. They add real value by helping us think strategically, and then apply that thinking to our deliverables. Their contributions go beyond design to understanding our business and how creative development and execution can help us be more effective in reaching our key audiences." Kim Kondraki, Vice President of Public Affairs, TIAA-CREF

LOCATION

Selbert Perkins Design Collaborative
200 Culver Boulevard
Playa del Rey, CA 90293
T: 310.822.5223
F: 310.822.5203
www.selbertperkinsdesign.com

SERVICES

- Brand Identity
- City/Streetscapes
- Naming Systems
- Product & Package Design

- Print Communications
- Public Art & Sculpture
- Signage & Wayfinding
- Web Communications

Photography by Anton Grassl

1. Los Angeles International Airport: Los Angeles, California

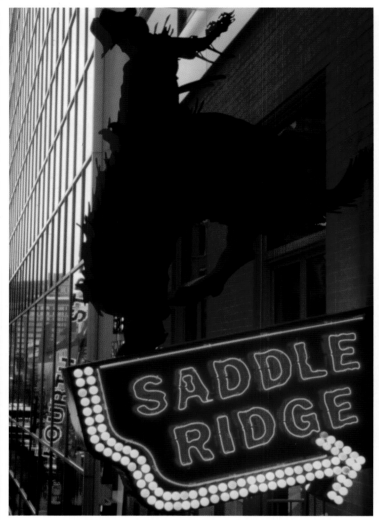

2. Fourth Street Live!: Louisville, Kentucky

3. Pacific Design Center: West Hollywood, California

5. East Fremont Street: Las Vegas, Nevada

Photography by Andrew Davey

7. *Marina Del Rey: Marina Del Rey, California*

8. World of Coca Cola: Atlanta, Georgia

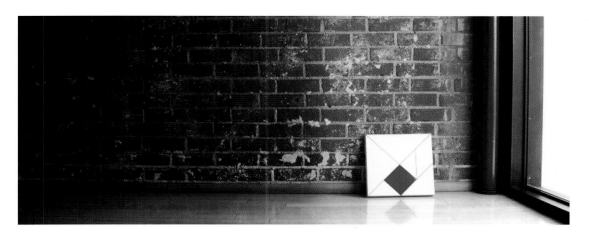

SooHoo Designers   1424 Marcelina Avenue, Torrance, CA 90501 310.381.0170
soohoodesign.com   shd@soohoodesign.com

At SooHoo Designers, everyday we are asked to put our creative talents into action. For us, sensitivity, imagination, innovation and elevation are the essential elements for a brand's success.

At SooHoo Designers, our discipline leads to high standards of quality. Our know-how is the fruit of our branding experience: experience in the markets, experience in developing concept and experience in continuously renewed creative approaches.

At SooHoo Designers, we believe brands are like people and take on human like traits. Like friends we have, the brands we associate with say something about us to others and maybe even to ourselves. When creating brands we ask: If this brand were a person, who would it be?

zoodiac™ tiger:
you're adventurous,
brave, energetic & often
unpredictable, but
very tender.

i'm adventurous

Zoodiac Logo

zoodiac™

i'm...

cleuer / spirited
strong / original
adventurous / perfect
caring / loyal
fiesty / pure
charming

zoodiac™

p.o. box 254, torrance, ca 90507
t / f 310 381 0154 e contact@zoodiac.net w zoodiac.net

i'm...

clever
strong
adventurous ✓
caring
fiesty ✓
charming
spirited
original
funny
perfect ✓
loyal
pure

zoodiac onesies

tiger
You're adventurous, brave, energetic and often unpredictable, but very tender.

100% cotton, imported. Silkscreened, ultra soft and roomy. Available in milk, cotton candy, sky and meadow colors.

captured!
adventurous tiger in milk flared tee

i'm adventurous

i'm adventurous

zoodiac bibs

monkey
You're funny, popular, spunky and often too mischievous, but very smart.

100% cotton, imported. Silkscreened, ultra soft and roomy. Available in milk, cotton candy, sky and meadow colors.

seen!
funny monkey in banana bib

i'm funny

i'm funny

Every business, product or institution has a promise, a personality, a story to tell. Our job is to help make that story resonate. Stoltze Design excels at helping our clients clarify their unique vision and project it into the world. By asking the right questions, we help unearth those distinctive personality traits and demonstrate how to creatively leverage them for maximum impact. Through an inclusive process based on thorough exploration and sound strategy, we create compelling communications that effectively articulate and reinforce the client's essence: their brand.

Stoltze Design offers a wide range of strategic design solutions including print, packaging and interactive media for a diverse group of demanding clients from business and culture. In a crowded market place, our process yields sophisticated, original results that elevate our clients above the visual fray.

07
08

PASSIONATE MUSIC MAKING WITHOUT BOUNDARIES

BOSTON

PHILHARMONIC
BENJAMIN ZANDER
conductor

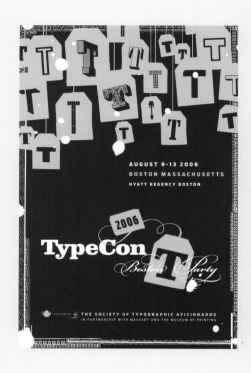

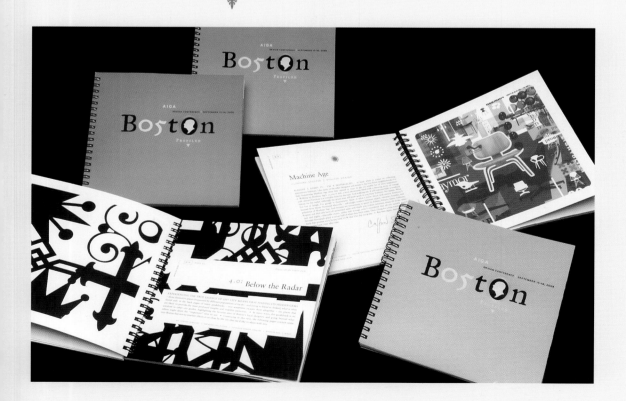

TypeCon T 2006
Boston T Party

AUGUST 9-13 2006 | BOSTON MASSACHUSETTS S{o}T A

The COOLIDGE CORNER THEATRE
presents
the FIRST ANNUAL

COOLIDGE AWARD HONORING
ZHANG YIMOU

DIRECTOR, Foreign Language Film
May 2004

WWW.COOLIDGE.ORG

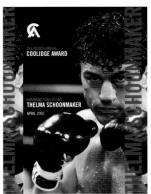

COOLIDGE
AWARD

Cakewalk/Home Studio
Opholio
Chelsea Pictures
Idiom

AIGA/Boston
MIT/MechE
Cakewalk

Shout Factory Records
MIT/BCS
Six Red Marbles

September Productions
Cakewalk/Project 5
Office Environments
MIT/SDM

Anarchy Club
Lunch TV
Fidelity Investments

Sussner Design Co.

The human hand dominates the Sussner Design Company (SDCo) brand image. A palm with four flexible fingers and one opposable thumb has obvious affinity with well-crafted, intelligent design work.

There's the personal approach, the human touch, the attention to detail and of course, the big, friendly "hiya" to clients willing and able to engage in a legitimate hand-in-hand partnership. At SDCo, "hands-on" & "collaborative" is not vacant marketing babble; they are the guidelines for every project and every client.

For Sussner Design Co., the hand represents a different shade of blue-collar work ethic. This shop makes a sincere effort to understand the realities of each client/partner.

The process of design discovery involves deep examination, open discussion, soulful intuition and divine intervention. The results need to jump up every morning, go to work and get the job done right.

Sussner Design Co. is a Minneapolis firm firmly planted since 1999. Originally, it was Derek Sussner behind the hand. Now the name "Sussner" represents a group of likeminded people working hand-in-hand (so to speak).

SUSSNER DESIGN CO.
212 3RD AVE N. SUITE 505
MINNEAPOLIS, MN 55401
612.339.2886
SUSSNER.COM

WELCOME TO CHASE FIELD

SECTIONS 200-300 and ALL SUITES ←

SECTIONS 116-145 ↑

- Advanced Tickets
- Guest Relations
- Team Store
- ATM

West Plaza

DIAMOND BACKS

Sussner Design Co. brings its game to Major League Baseball's Arizona Diamondbacks. The assignment: Take the DBacks' new brand palette and integrate it functionally, efficiently and dynamically into physical elements of their stadium, Chase Field.

SDCo created a full-on experience for game attendees that delivered tasteful consistency across a diverse range of components. From branding signage that required a special level of flexibility to wayfinding signage that demanded go-here intuitiveness on a long-term basis.

The ultimate result was a clean, fresh look that vividly shapes and informs every visit to Chase Field. SDCo produced a thoughtful, smart and perfectly aligned brand extension that took the DiamondBacks' visual image to the next level. Major League designing on a major scale.

480 FEET*
FROM THIS POINT
TO HOME PLATE
*or 80 Orlando Hudsons,
or 2,010 baseballs,
or 960 hot dogs

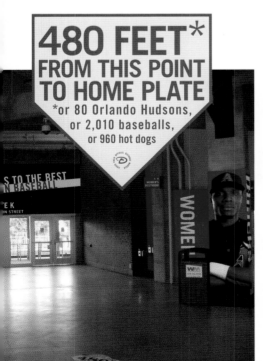

BRINGING THE "TARGET" TO TARGET COMMERCIAL INTERIORS

AN ANNUAL FOR THE ANIMALS VIA THE ANIMAL HUMANE SOCIETY

BEYOND DAILY REQUIREMENTS FOR LIFE TIME FITNESS MULTIVITAMINS

PAINTING A GRAPHIC PORTRAIT OF INTERNATIONAL WALL DESIGNS

HOW DID YOU GET HERE?

AIGA
the professional association for design

AIGA Minnesota

AIGA MINNESOTA
DESIGN CAMP
OCTOBER 6-8 2006
GRAND VIEW LODGE
REGISTER ONLINE STARTING AUGUST 1, 2006
AIGAMINN.ORG/DESIGNCAMP

AIGA MINNESOTA DESIGN CAMP
GRAND VIEW LODGE

DID DESIGN CAMP MATERIALS
MOVED TO BEARD AVE.
GOT NEW HAIRCUT
SWITCHED TO DECAF
BOUGHT TUMS   INVENTED VELCRO
GREW A BEARD   LEFT TOWN
GOT NOSE JOB   D-I-V-O-R-C-E   TOOK DAY OFF
GREED   9/11   SOLD ART   YIELDED   I VOTED
ZAGGED   ESPRESSO   LEFT EARLY
SEX   HAD A BABY   VIAGRA
WOKE UP WITH ODD RASH   SHOT IN B&W   SENT PO
MADE A DUPLICATE   MET DESIGN IDOL
CUT WINDOW   DESIGNED BY SUSSNER DESIGN CO.   CALL
ERB   STAYED UP 42 HOURS STRAIGHT   THOUGHT TOO MUCH
OLVED MYSTERY   DELETED
COPY WRITTER JEFF MUELLER   TOOK THE STAIRS
ADOPTED TWINS   GAVE STR
PHONE   FELL DOWN THE STAIRS
BOUGHT NEW PHOTOSHOP
FIRST CLIENT
SOLD FIRST ILLUST
SCREENED T-SHIRT

Activities
MIXER DINNER
MAC LAB
KARAOKE
PAINTING
VENDOR EXPO
BONFIRE N S'MORES
MORNING MEDITATION
ENTERTAINMENT
DEVIL'S FLYING MACHINE
BREAKFAST PUZZLES

A WORK IN PROCESS
AIGA MN DESIGN CAMP 2006

Speakers

DESIGN CAMP
Derek Sussner
NOW IN PROCESS
DAY 1   DAY 2   DAY 3

TAPPED BY AMERICAN INSTITUTE OF GRAPHIC ARTS MINNESOTA FOR ALL THINGS DESIGN CAMP

CREATING THE IMAGE FOR FULL-SERVICE PRINTER, REFLECTIONS

FROM THE GROUND UP WITH FUNCTIONAL FURNITURE DEVELOPER, HERCKE

SUSSNER DESIGN COMPANY, REFLECTIONS 24, READY CREDIT, AIGA MN, REFLECTIONS, SUSSNER DESIGN COMPANY, HERCKE INTERNATIONAL, FLAIRE PRINT, THE SUCCESS GROUP, RADISSON, RADISSON, VOYAGEUR OUTWARD BOUND, VOYAGEUR OUTWARD BOUND, REFLECTIONS, TARGET COMMERCIAL INTERIORS, LORENZO'S HAIR SALON, SWING SCIENCE GOLF, JOE SCHAAK, KEYS TO..., THUNDERBIRD BUILDING INTERIORS

TOKY Branding+Design
3139 Olive Street
St. Louis, MO 63103
(314) 534 2000
www.toky.com

EST
1929

every
possibility

every
desire

IT'S ALL IN THE CHASE

VISIT OUR SALES CENTER. CLICK HERE FOR MORE INFORMATION. | LATEST NEWS ■ SEND TO A FRIEND

VISIT THE CHASE PARK PLAZA HOTEL SITE

THE SKY ABOVE YOU.

A FOREST BELOW YOU.

YOUR DAY *behind you.*

It's all in The Chase.

THE PRIVATE RESIDENCES
AT THE
Chase Park Plaza

For more information call 314.633.3400 | *or visit* WWW.CHASERESIDENCES.COM

THE PRIVATE RESIDENCES
AT THE
Chase Park Plaza

THE PRIVATE RESIDENCES | YOUR PLACE IN HISTORY | PREMIER LOCATION | REQUEST ADDITIONAL INFORMATION

every
possibility

IT'S ALL IN THE CHASE

VISIT OUR SALES CENTER. CLICK HERE FOR MORE INFORMATION. | LATEST NEWS ■ SEND TO A FRIEND

HOK Architects

Web Site Redesign
Brochures

theHOKPlanningGroup

Urban Redevelopment

theHOKPlanningGroup

New Urban Studio

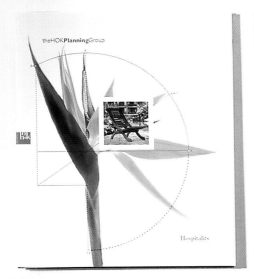

theHOKPlanningGroup

Hospitality

theHOKPlanningGroup

Commercial

theHOKPlanningGroup

Education

theHOKPlanningGroup

Community

theHOKPlanningGroup

Planning, Landscape Architecture and Urban Design

theHOKPlanningGroup

Corporate

theHOKPlanningGroup

Transportation

THIS IS
PASSION.
THIS IS
DESIRE.
THIS IS
MAGIC,
ROMANCE,
LAUGHTER,
REVENGE,
BETRAYAL,
JEALOUSY,
DECEIT,
ENVY,
INTRIGUE,
AND
LOVE,
SWEET LOVE.

OPERA THEATRE OF SAINT LOUIS 2004

CARMEN   CAVALLERIA RUSTICANA/SISTER ANGELICA   THE SECRET MARRIAGE   NIXON IN CHINA

JANE EYRE
THE AMERICAN PREMIERE
MICHAEL BERKELEY
(2000)

STREET SCENE
KURT WEILL (1947)

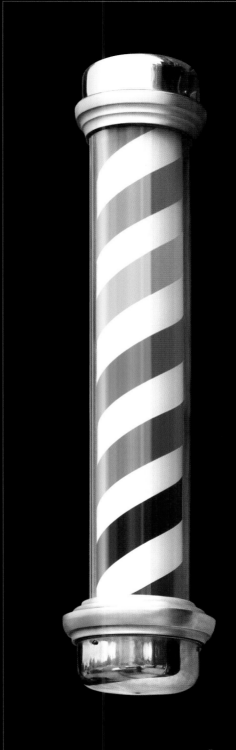

**Opera Theatre
of Saint Louis**

Brand Identity
Marketing Brochures
Season Posters
Season Titles
Print Advertising
Television
Radio
Web Site

The Barber of Seville

A Presentation Of OPERA THEATRE OF SAINT LOUIS To Benefit
THE HUMAN RIGHTS CAMPAIGN And Their Work Toward LGBT Equality

TUESDAY | JUNE 13TH | 7PM SHARP

**Bissinger's
Handcrafted Chocolatier**

Corporate Identity
Brand Identity
Packaging
Business Papers
Print Collateral
Catalogs
Web Site

**The Smokehouse
Market**

Brand Identity
Packaging
Business Papers
Web Site

Tompertdesign
514 High Street, Atelier
Palo Alto, CA 94301
(650) 323-0365
www.tompertdesign.com

Our award-winning work exhibits a distinctive balance of emotion and function—dynamic designs that are open to imagination and interpretation while fulfilling their purpose. Capturing the essence of the brand, our forward-looking design solutions are unique and lasting representations of our clients and their products.

Our full-service capabilities are in brand identity and corporate communications, from logo and collateral design to website development. With a cutting-edge culture and technical savvy that is equaled by our respect and love for the craftsmanship of print, we excel in smart and elegant integration of traditional and new media.

Over the last 15 years, we have served talented entrepreneurs, start-ups and established companies in a lively mix of industries, from hi-tech and biotech to fashion and non-profit. Our work has been recognized in books, annuals and competitions including HOW, PRINT, Graphis, American Corporate Identity and Communication Arts.

Meli Meli

A unique children's clothing line for little girls marked by its whimsical and decidedly vintage approach to fabrics and silhouettes.

Logotype

Lifestyle & Product Photography

Letterpress Stationery

Garment Tags

Clothing Labels

Line Sheets

Look Books

Promotions

Direct Mail

Website

Global Fund for Women

A non-profit foundation using innovative approaches to advance women's rights worldwide.

Logo
Stationery
Environment
Collateral
Direct Mail
Email Newsletter
Advertising
Annual Report
Web 2.0 with CMS
    and online donation

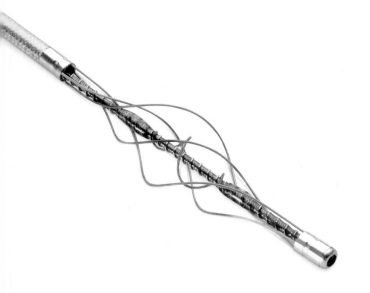

DVT Treatment Advances

Clinical trial recruitment and information package, educating physicians and patients about DVT (Deep Vein Thrombosis) and emerging treatment options for blood clot removal.

Identity
Collateral Material
Slideshow
Website
Tradeshow Graphics

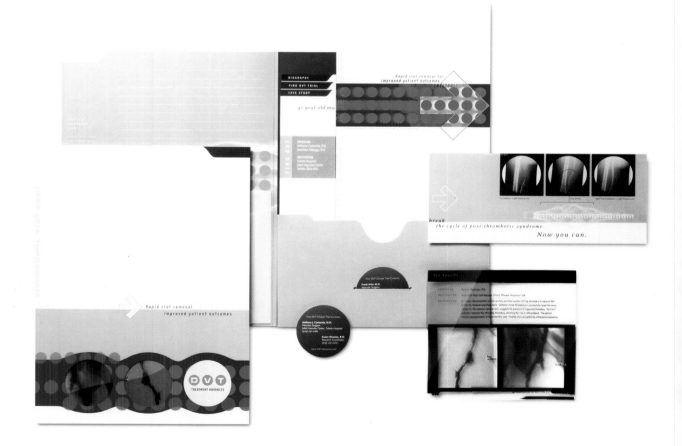

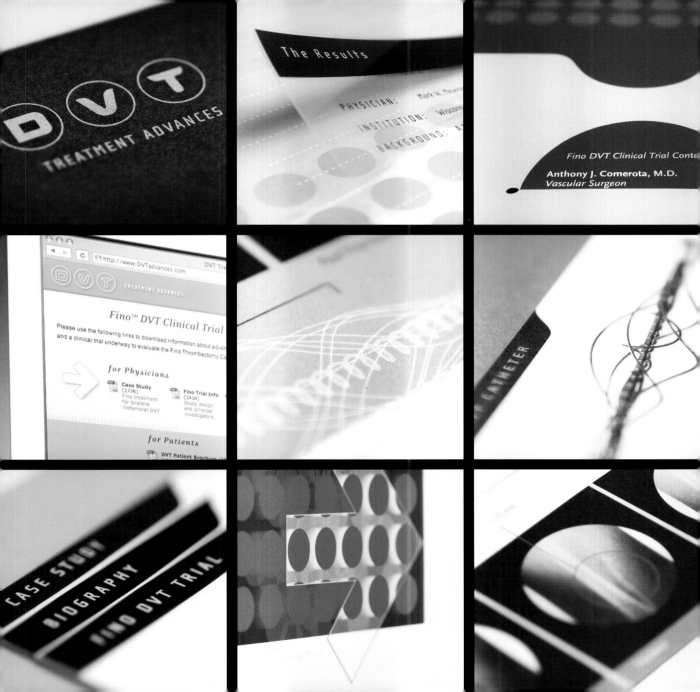

Protein Discovery
Laboratory systems for pharmaceutical and life science research specifically in the area of proteomics.

ThermoForte
Advanced thermal backfill material used to keep under–ground power cables cool.

OsteoCorp
Developer of drugs that reverse the skeletal thinning caused by osteoporosis by stimulating re-growth of new bone tissue.

Raygun Studio
Offering creative retouching, photorealistic 3D modeling and rendering, general imaging magic.

VeraLight
Medical device company offering screening solutions using laser light for non-invasive diabetes checks.

Scimagix
Technology to search large databases of scientific images not only by keywords, but image content—think color, texture, patterns and spatial relationships.

LifeSignals
A web-based platform for collection, analysis and digital transmission of heart data.

Seewolf
Yacht tour and charter service organizing adventure vacations in the Mediterranean sea.

Visual Asylum

We believe in creating memorable brand identities by developing a unique "visual language" which defines and establishes the appropriate personality for an organization, a product or service and manages the ways in which that personification is communicated. Branding begins when a logo is placed into an environment. We create the appropriate tools with which to build the environments; name, logo, color palettes, patterns, typographic styling, photography and illustration. The environment then evokes the brands personality.

www.visualasylum.com

205 WEST DATE SAN DIEGO CA
T 619 - 233-9633 F 619- 233-9637

SCOTT FORESMAN

HISTORY-SOCIAL SCIENCE FOR CALIFORNIA
LEARN AND WORK
K
TEACHER ORGANIZER

HISTORY-SOCIAL SCIENCE FOR CALIFORNIA
TIME AND PLACE
1
TEACHER ORGANIZER

HISTORY-SOCIAL SCIENCE FOR CALIFORNIA
THEN AND NOW
2
TEACHER ORGANIZER

HISTORY-SOCIAL SCIENCE FOR CALIFORNIA
OUR COMMUNITIES
3
TEACHER ORGANIZER

HISTORY-SOCIAL SCIENCE FOR CALIFORNIA
OUR CALIFORNIA
4
TEACHER ORGANIZER

1 California K-5 Social Studies Program > **2** Teacher Binder > **3** Teacher Binder and Student Wookbooks > **4** Student Wookbooks

1 Exterior Signage and Menu Board > **2** Menu > **3** Interior Signage > **4** Menu Board

1 Exterior Signage > **2** Signage > **3** Menu Board > **4** Illustration > **5** Beer Logos

AIGA San Diego Y Design Conference > **1** Stage Design > **2** Conference Collateral

Wages Design, Inc.

Wages Design, Inc.
887 W. Marietta Street
Suite S-111
Atlanta, GA 30318
404.876.0874
www.wagesdesign.com
info@wagesdesign.com

Tried, Tested and True: Wages Design
After Nearly Three Decades in Business, Wages Knows What Works — and What Doesn't

Since 1979, Wages Design has been bringing Atlanta, the Southeast and national audiences some of the finest branding, corporate identity, print collateral, package and new media design in the United States. It is a seasoned and mature creative agency, with nine staff members, including four full time graphic designers, two full-time account directors, a creative director and a director of new media. The average tenure of the staff (excluding Bob Wages and the venerable, beloved Beth Perpall) is over ten years.

The Wages process is simple and effective: dedicate adequate resources to research the client, its competitors and the marketing challenge ahead. Use that knowledge to define clear design criteria. Ask every designer on staff to work up fresh concepts based upon the approved criteria.

By creating a "contest among peers," agency thinking and talent is maximized while offering clients a wide variety of options.

"We offer clients the greatest possible creative options and designers who can apply the selected creative direction to whatever marketing vehicle or tactic required," explains Bob Wages. "This includes, identity, collateral, direct mail, and new media. This team is so experienced and deep that they remove the time-consuming and wasteful trial and error process that can occur at less mature shops."

Is Wages making virtue out of necessity? No. The proof is in the work, a legacy of finished product second to none, a portfolio that remains fresh and effective, no matter the age, the name or the heritage of the individual designer most involved in its creation.

Besides, a little salt and pepper can add a lot of flavor.

By Matthew Porter
Design writer and critic for Communication Arts and STEP Magazines

CBL Properties,
a mall real estate developer

Executed the marketing
campaign, which included
identity, advertising, print
collateral, and web site
development.

Makeup's gone existential

and aren't we glad. The dark red lips and pancake face of years past have yielded to a wild profusion of looks, textures, skin tones and full-body treatments. The beauty of Rex is that we can imitate and accentuate whatever brand visage you want to project. To the rextreme.

exceptional
quality

rextensive
quality control

www.rexcorp.com

rex

rexceptional
creativity

rexc

Rex Corporation,
consumer packaging printer

Developed a marketing and
promotional campaign theme
through package and print
collateral design.

This page:

Antron® carpet fiber,
*a division of INVISTA and the
leader in commercial carpet fiber*

Through ongoing web support,
the Flash intro is redesigned every
quarter to promote new products
or themes, like Fiber Effects,
Aesthetics, and Brilliance (which
included a direct mail promotion).

Opposite page:

Mi Casa Tortillas,
*a division of Flowers Foods and
a leading producer/marketer
of packaged bakery foods*

Redesigned the overall Mi Casa
identity and packaging and
then rolled out the new tortilla
packaging nationwide.

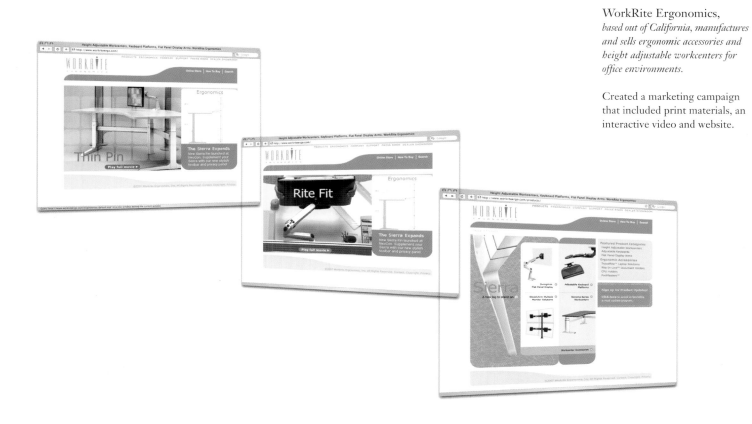

WorkRite Ergonomics, *based out of California, manufactures and sells ergonomic accessories and height adjustable workcenters for office environments.*

Created a marketing campaign that included print materials, an interactive video and website.

DATE DUE

JUL 27 2011	
JAN 26 2012	
	& TAYLOR